Endorsements

This is the hottest message on the planet!
—Tom Grinner, Gateway Broadcasting

It will revolutionize the church.
—Pastor Reb Bradley, CA

The best thing I have ever heard!
—Pastor Wayne Welborn, MO

I began to weep as I saw the importance of this message.
—Pastor Ken Armstrong, CA

I am a 52-year-old pastor. I have had my own TV program, but when I heard this teaching, I felt as though I knew nothing. It shocked me!
—A pastor from Oklahoma

Hell's Best Kept Secret has completely destroyed my theology. What was first anger toward you caused me to search the Scripture, and has now turned to a sincere thank you.
—Pastor Jerod McPherson

Today I listened to *Hell's Best Kept Secret* for the first time. It changed the way I look at everything. I was blind to it until today.   —Scott Wilson, KY

I listened to *Hell's Best Kept Secret* 250 times!
—Pastor Chris Stockwell

You will want to play and replay this message until you understand it!   —David Wilkerson

Hell's Best Kept Secret is a message every congregation needs to hear.
—Tom Elliff, President of the Southern Baptist Convention (1996–1998)

After a thousand revivals and area crusades, I have used a lot of soulwinning materials. *Hell's Best Kept Secret* is the greatest single tool I have ever found.   —Larry Taylor, Evangelist

Ray Comfort brings us a word that cuts to the core of man's spiritual dilemma. As we pray for revival and wonder what God's waiting for, we need to seriously consider this message. To ignore it puts us in spiritual peril.   —Terry Meeuwsen, Co-host, *The 700 Club*

hell's best kept
SECRET

RAY COMFORT

**WHITAKER
HOUSE**

Unless otherwise indicated, all Scripture quotations are taken from the *New King James Version* (NKJV), © 1979, 1980, 1982 by Thomas Nelson, Inc. Used by permission. All rights reserved.
Scripture quotations marked (KJV) are taken from the King James Version of the Bible.
Scripture quotations marked (TLB) are from *The Living Bible,* © 1971 by Tyndale House Publishers, Wheaton, Illinois. Used by permission.
Scripture quotations marked (AMP) are taken from *The Amplified New Testament* © 1958, 1987 by The Lockman Foundation. Used by permission.
Editorial note: Even at the cost of violating grammatical rules, we have chosen not to capitalize the name satan and related names.

HELL'S BEST KEPT SECRET

Ray Comfort
P.O. Box 1172
Bellflower, CA 90706
www.raycomfort.com

ISBN: 0-88368-277-X
Printed in the United States of America
© 1989 by Ray Comfort

Whitaker House
30 Hunt Valley Circle
New Kensington, PA 15068

Library of Congress Cataloging-in-Publication Data

Comfort, Ray.
    Hell's best kept secrets / Ray Comfort.
        p. cm.
    Includes bibliographical references.
    ISBN 0-88368-277-X (pbk.)
    1. Evangelistic work. 2. Law and gospel.   I. Title.
    BV3793 .C635 2002
    269'.2—dc21   2001006823

1 2 3 4 5 6 7 8 9 10 11 12 / 10 09 08 07 06 05 04 03 02

Dedication

To Pastor Garry Ansdell and his lovely wife Denise, for their desire to see souls soundly saved, and for their kindness in helping us to make America our new home. To Dan and Evelyn Eastep, Christopher Hromek, Mark Okasaki, Neil O'Donnell, Keith and Cathy White, Whitaker House, Dan Skomerza, and Dave Boyd, for their love of the truth, and to my wife, Sue (my best friend and partner in the Gospel).

Contents

Preface 9

1. The Love, Joy, Peace Gospel 11
2. Hell's Best Kept Secret 23
3. The Jesus Technique 31
4. Pushing for Commitment? 43
5. The Forgotten Key 53
6. No Anointing—No Results 67
7. Fired Up! 77
8. The Way of the Salesman........................ 87
9. When and Where to Witness 101
10. Let's Buy the World Lunch 111
11. Why the Law Works 119
12. Ten Steps to Conviction........................ 133
13. Time to Talk about Jesus....................... 143
14. Who Are the Backsliders?..................... 155
15. Success Comes in "Cans" 165
16. You've Got What It Takes 179

Appendix: Questions and Answers.............. 195
About the Author.......................................205
Suggested Reading 206

Preface

Recently, twenty thousand Christian men set aside a day to pray for revival. Motivated by a concern for souls, they left behind their daily pleasures and denied themselves for the sake of the Gospel. Talking to God about men, however, is often easier than talking to men about God.

What if those twenty thousand men combined action with their prayers? What if each of them cried, "O God, give me just one soul a year"? If the one they led to the Lord prayed that same prayer, in just twelve years, 174,000,000 souls would be saved!

Most Christians don't pray that sort of prayer. We pass the buck of evangelism to the evangelist. But Jesus commanded all His disciples to *"go into all the world and preach the gospel to every creature"* (Mark 16:15). Biblically, the buck stops with each of us. Every Christian has a moral responsibility to evangelize this dying world.

In August 1982, God saw my own feeble (and somewhat futile) efforts to reach the lost. He graciously reached down, took the blinders from my eyes, and revealed to me the "key of knowledge"—the key to revival. This key—hell's best kept secret—has been hidden from the church for generations.

This golden, but neglected, key unlocks the door to the souls of men. Once you grasp this biblical principle, you will share your faith with new zeal. No longer will you sit in powerlessness, frustrated while sinners pass you by, sinking into hell. Your witness and evangelistic efforts will never be the same.

Please allow me, with the assistance of God, to pass that priceless key to you through the pages of this book.

1

The Love, Joy, Peace Gospel

Evangelical success is at an all-time low. Modern evangelism, from large campaigns to small gospel meetings, boasts only a 20 percent holding rate.

How effective are our present-day evangelical methods when they create eighty backsliders for every one hundred "decisions for Jesus"? Some are even less effective than that—one recent campaign reported having a 92 percent backsliding rate!

The September 1977 issue of *Eternity Magazine* reported the results of an evangelistic crusade that involved 178 churches. Out of 4,106 decisions, only 3 percent joined a local church. That series of meetings created 3,981 backsliders! (More up-to-date statistics are hard to come by. Understandably, they are not published with much enthusiasm.)

I did read that, in 1987, a Luis Palau crusade reported 6,000 decisions. Yet, despite intense follow-up and counsel, within the first three months, 947 had already backslidden.

To those who have a burden for the lost, like Luis Palau, Billy Graham, and many gifted evangelists around the world, these statistics are not just bad news—they are heartrending! While evangelicals run around in ever-decreasing circles, 140,000 souls die every day.

Why No Brokenness?

As a young evangelist I would plead with sinners, begging them to accept Christ. When one would respond, I was overjoyed. But in the back of my mind I knew there was an 80 percent chance that he would backslide.

To test the sincerity of a potential convert who came to the altar, I began to approach each sinner in a gestapo-like manner. When I felt he was sincere, I would lead him in the most genuine prayer I could muster, "Dear God, I am a sinner. Cleanse me, wash me."

As we prayed, I would keep one eye open. Although obviously sincere, sinners repeated it flippantly. Then I would lower my voice and almost tearfully affirm, "I believe that Jesus died on the cross in my place." Still there was no sign of sorrow for sin, no contrition, and no brokenness!

What was the problem? The sinner was 100 percent—he sincerely wanted the love, joy, peace, happiness, and fulfillment that supposedly come from being a Christian. His response was merely a test to see if the claims are true.

Sinners were not fleeing from the wrath to come. Why? Because I hadn't mentioned there was any wrath to come. Potential converts showed no genuine repentance because I hadn't given them reason to repent.

Who Needs a Parachute?

The way we present the Gospel determines the kind of response the sinner makes. Let me illustrate.

Two men are seated in a plane. A stewardess gives the first man a parachute and instructs him to put it on because it will "improve his flight."

Not understanding how a parachute could possibly improve his flight, the first passenger is a little skeptical. Finally he decides to see if the claim is true. After strapping on the parachute, he notices its burdensome weight, and he has difficulty sitting upright. Consoling himself with the promise of a better flight, our first passenger decides to give it a little time.

Because he's the only one wearing a parachute, some of the other passengers begin smirking at him, which only adds to his humiliation. Unable to stand it any longer, our friend slumps in his seat, unstraps the parachute, and throws it to the floor. Disillusionment and bitterness fill his heart because, as far as he is concerned, he was told a lie.

Another stewardess gives the second man a parachute, *but listen to her instructions.* She tells him to put it on because at any moment he will be jumping out of the plane at 25,000 feet.

Our second passenger gratefully straps the parachute on. He doesn't notice its weight upon his shoulders or that he can't sit upright. His mind is consumed with the thought of what would happen to him if he jumped without it. When other passengers laugh at him, he thinks, "You won't be laughing when you're falling to the ground!"

Inoculated Backsliders

Let's now analyze the motive and the result of each passenger's experience.

The first man's motive for putting on the parachute was solely to improve his flight. As a result, he was humiliated by the passengers, disillusioned by an unkept promise, and embittered against the stewardess who gave it to him. As far as he is concerned, he will never put one of those things on his back again.

The second man put on the parachute to escape the danger of the upcoming jump. Because he knew what would happen to him without it, he had a deep-rooted joy and peace in his heart. Knowing he was saved from certain death gave him the ability to withstand the mockery of the other passengers. His attitude toward the stewardess who gave him the parachute was one of heartfelt gratitude.

Now listen to what the contemporary gospel message says: "Put on the Lord Jesus Christ; He will give you love, joy, peace, and fulfillment." In other words, *He will improve your flight.* In an experimental fashion, the sinner puts on the Savior to see if these claims are so.

What does he get? Temptation, tribulation, and persecution. The other passengers mock his decision. So what does he do? He takes off the Lord Jesus Christ; he is offended for the Word's sake; he is disillusioned and embittered, and quite rightly so.

He was promised peace, joy, and fulfillment, and all he got were trials and humiliation. His bitterness is directed at those who gave him the "Good News." His latter end is worse than the first—another inoculated, bitter backslider!

The apostle Peter acted in misguided zeal when he tried to dismember the Roman servant in the Garden of Gethsemane. Many misguided Christians are also cutting off the ears of potential hearers. Once sinners think they have given it a try, they no longer have an ear for the Gospel.

Why are sinners turned off and tuned out? Because we no longer preach the full message of the Gospel. We have omitted the key to genuine repentance—the Law of God. The apostle Paul said, *"I would not have known sin **except through the law"*** (Romans 7:7, emphasis added).

Listen to these words from Spurgeon:

> Lower the Law, and you dim the light by which man perceives his guilt. This is a very serious loss to the sinner, rather than a gain; for it lessens the likelihood of his conviction and conversion....I say you have deprived the Gospel of its ablest auxiliary [most powerful weapon] when you have set aside the Law. You have taken away from it the schoolmaster that is to bring men to Christ....*They will never accept grace till they tremble before a just and holy Law.* Therefore, the Law serves a most necessary and blessed purpose, and it must not be removed from its place.

When the sinner sees the awful consequences of breaking the Law of God—that he cannot escape the certainty of judgment—he will see his need to put on the Lord Jesus Christ. When we preach future punishment by the Law, the sinner comes to Christ solely to flee from "the wrath to come."

Instead of preaching that Jesus "improves the flight," we must warn men about the inevitable jump. Everyone must pass through the door of death.

> *It is appointed for men to die once, but after this the judgment.*   (Hebrews 9:27)

But doesn't Christianity offer the abundant life? You bet it does! Peace and joy are legitimate fruits of the Spirit. But we do sinners an injustice by enticing them with only the *benefits* of salvation. Our misguided efforts only result in sinners coming to Christ with an impure motive void of repentance.

Remember why the second passenger had joy and peace? Because he knew what that parachute was going to save him from. In the same way, the true convert has joy and peace in believing because he knows that the righteousness of Christ will deliver him from the wrath that is to come. *"The kingdom of God is...righteousness and peace and joy in the Holy Spirit"* (Romans 14:17). Why is righteousness coupled with peace and joy? Because *"riches do not profit in the day of wrath, but righteousness delivers from death"* (Proverbs 11:4).

Man-Centered Preaching

Now let's take a look at an unfortunate incident on board the plane. During some unexpected turbulence, the stewardess accidentally drops a cup of hot coffee onto the lap of our second passenger.

What is his reaction? Does he cry out in pain, then rip the parachute off his back in anger? No! He didn't put it on for any other reason than the jump. In fact, he doesn't even relate the incident to his parachute. Instead, it only makes him cling more tightly to his hope of salvation and even look forward to the jump!

If we put on Christ to flee the wrath to come, when tribulation strikes we won't get angry at God. Why should we?

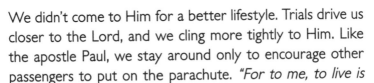

The Love, Joy, Peace Gospel

We didn't come to Him for a better lifestyle. Trials drive us closer to the Lord, and we cling more tightly to Him. Like the apostle Paul, we stay around only to encourage other passengers to put on the parachute. *"For to me, to live is Christ, and to die is gain"* (Philippians 1:21).

Sadly, multitudes of professing Christians lose their joy when the flight gets bumpy. They are the product of "man-centered" preaching.

Because the Law is rarely used in modern-day evangelism, many pastors are frustrated and make the Gospel "man-centered" in an effort to attract converts. They don't see men and women embracing the Good News, so they turn to man-made methods.

Instead of *driving* the fish to the nets using the Law, they try to *attract* them by holding up only the benefits of salvation. Let me give an example of a typical altar call:

> Come to Jesus. Won't you give your heart to Him?
> He loves you and died on the cross for you. He wants
> to give you love, joy, and peace. He will make your life
> happy and give you what you've been looking for.

Ministers gently woo sinners to the altar with the "every eye closed and every head bowed" approach. Then, as the music gently plays, the preacher asks, "Why not ask the person next to you to come with you so Jesus can make him happy?"

An Invitation or a Command?

Instead of desperate sinners knocking on the door of heaven, we incorrectly paint a picture of Jesus pleading at the heart of the sinner. This type of "invitation" gives the impression that the sinner will be doing God a favor if he responds. The Gospel is not an *invitation,* because invitations can be politely turned down without fear of reprisal. Scripture says, *"God...**commands** all men everywhere to repent"* (Acts 17:30, emphasis added).

We would never dare quote some of the following verses to encourage someone to come to Christ:

> *All who desire to live godly in Christ Jesus will suffer persecution.* (2 Timothy 3:12)

> *We must through many tribulations enter the kingdom of God.* (Acts 14:22)

> *Many are the afflictions of the righteous.* (Psalm 34:19)

> *In the world you will have tribulation.* (John 16:33)

Neither would we mention the sufferings of the apostle Paul—the stonings, perils, and shipwrecks he endured. Why, it's hard enough to get converts when we hold up the good things of the Gospel!

We try, in our evangelical zeal, to *argue* sinners into the kingdom by appealing to their intellect. We attempt to *scare* them into heaven by "666 campaigns." We try to *seduce* them into the kingdom by telling them that Jesus will make them happy. In fact, we use every method to bring people to Christ except the method God has ordained—the Law!

How to Fill a Church

Let's turn the spotlight inward for a moment. Do we preach a man-centered, "easy" Gospel because we want to see more people saved or because we know the consequences? Are we like the mother who won't discipline a naughty child because she doesn't like the feeling she gets when she does it? She places her immediate concern over the long-term welfare of her child.

Nathan may have felt sorry for King David as he cringed under the weight of the prophet's words, but Nathan had to obey God—not his feelings. David's eternal welfare was at stake. Better the sinner be offended in order to repent, than to enjoy the pleasures of sin for a season and be cast into everlasting fire. Where does the heart of our concern lie—with the fate of the sinner or with our own comfort?

The sinner hides *behind* the bush of sin. But we beat *around* the bush rather than beat the bush for fear of disturbing him. Yet the day will come when every sinner is flushed out.

Some Christians innocently ask, "Why not preach a 'man-centered' Gospel if it gets people 'saved'?" We can preach a man-centered Gospel and get results; we may even fill our churches. But adding a soul to *a* church does not necessarily mean that a soul has been added to *the* church. A decision for Christ doesn't necessarily mean a soul for Christ.

I attended one service where a challenge was made to accept Christ, but the Law of God was not mentioned. A young man stood up and briskly walked to the altar. He stepped to the platform, turned around, and smiled at the congregation. As I looked at him, I didn't see any outward sign of brokenness, guilt, or contrition. He wasn't fleeing to Christ for mercy. A short time later, he backslid.

Unlike this young man, some don't slide back into the world. Instead, church becomes no different than a social club. These new converts make plenty of friends; there are regular activities and no fees. Unfortunately, they also have no burden for souls, no real hunger for the Word, no zeal for God, and no *lasting* fruit. A "man-centered" Gospel can fill your church with this type of "conversion."

P. T. Forsyth has accurately observed:

> Our churches are full of the nicest, kindest people who have never known the despair of guilt or the breathless wonder of forgiveness.

I am not against altar calls. Nothing is wrong with responding to an altar call, but *what* sinners are responding to determines its effectiveness.

Hot or Cold?

There are only two kinds of Christians—"cold" and refreshing, or "hot" and stimulating. All the rest will be spewed out of the mouth of Christ on Judgment Day.

> *I know your works, that you are neither cold nor hot. I could wish you were cold or hot. So then, because you are lukewarm, and neither cold nor hot, I will vomit you out of My mouth.*
>
> (Revelation 3:15–16)

Soft-selling the Gospel is the tragedy of modern evangelism. Its massive casualty rate leaves multitudes in the "lukewarm" bracket and sours the untaught to the truths of true commitment. How can we turn the tide and restore credibility to our conversion rates? Let's stop soft-selling the Gospel and tell sinners how it is!

In the chapters ahead we will took at why and how to preach the Law effectively—not harshly. We'll show how you can bring sinners to repentance and see them soundly saved by presenting the truth of the Gospel with love and compassion.

2

Hell's Best Kept Secret

In typical prodigal fashion, a young man left his hometown to find life in the big city. He borrowed a fast car and, after having a few drinks, decided to impress those in his quiet hometown with its horsepower. With the accelerator pushed to the floor, tires squealing, and horn blaring, the car roared through the town at the dangerous speed of sixty miles per hour.

The townspeople were terrified. No such incident had ever occurred in their isolated village. In fact, since the townspeople owned so few cars, they had no law against speeding. As far as our speedster was concerned, he hadn't broken the law—because there wasn't one!

Immediately the town council gathered and passed a law stating that thirty miles per hour was the maximum speed within the town. Imprisonment or a fine of no less than one hundred dollars for every mile per hour over the speed limit would be imposed upon any transgressors of the law.

On his return trip through the town, our speedster decided to pull the same prank. Much to his shock and dismay, the newly elected traffic officer pulled him over and booked him for speeding at sixty miles per hour.

To his shame, the young man found himself in court, standing before his own father, the town's only judge. His father could not let his emotional tie to his son pervert justice, so he imposed the sentence demanded by the law—a three thousand dollar fine or imprisonment. Having no money and no words of defense, the youth was led away to jail.

Later that same day, the father arrived at the cell block, unlocked the door, and told his son he was free to go. In disbelief the young man listened to his father's amazing story. The quiet, older man explained that he had raised the three thousand dollars by selling numerous prized possessions.

It was hard for the son to believe his father loved him that much, yet he was humbled and filled with tremendous gratitude at the same time. The two embraced as they never had before, wept tears of joy, and walked off together in a newfound relationship bonded in love.

Why the Law?

Can you see what the law did for our speedster? The law showed him the depth of his lawlessness. Common sense told him he was doing wrong, but the law showed him just how wrong he was.

Do you fully understand the function of the Law of God for humanity? What does God's Word say about the use of the Law in preaching the Gospel?

1. The Law shows us our guilt before God and stops us from justifying ourselves.

Now we know that whatever the law says, it says to those who are under the law, that every mouth may

*be stopped, and all the world may become guilty
before God.*   (Romans 3:19)

2. The Law brings to us the knowledge of sin.

*Therefore by the deeds of the law no flesh will be
justified in His sight, for by the law is the knowledge
of sin.*   (Romans 3:20)

3. The Law defines sin. The apostle Paul didn't even know what sin was, until the Law told him!

*What shall we say then? Is the law sin? Certainly
not! On the contrary, I would not have known sin
except through the law. For I would not have known
covetousness unless the law had said, "You shall not
covet."*   (Romans 7:7)

4. The Law was designed for the very purpose of bringing men and women to Christ.

*Therefore the law was our tutor to bring us to
Christ, that we might be justified by faith.*
                    (Galatians 3:24)

Just as the law left our speedster in a helpless state
before the judge, with no means of payment and no words
of justification, so the Law of God leaves the sinner with no
means of payment before the Judge of the universe.

*None of them can by any means redeem his brother,
nor give to God a ransom for him; for the redemption of their souls is costly.*   (Psalm 49:7–8)

The Law doesn't help anybody; it just leaves us in a helpless state before God.

So What?

Have you ever wondered why the sinner isn't moved by Calvary? His mind wanders, and he almost yawns as you share how the Son of God shed His blood to pay for our sins. "So what?" he thinks. He isn't moved to tears like the saint who knows the depth of his lawlessness and the tremendous pardon that God has granted him.

For the answer to this mystery, let's go back to our speedster. If he was ignorant of the *standard,* the *certainty,* and the *severity* of the law, then the good news of his father's paying the fine would make no sense to him. The outcome would have been quite different if he hadn't been told that the law had set the speed limit at thirty miles per hour; that once he was arrested he could not escape; and that the fine was severe.

Imagine the traffic officer hailing this young man from his high-speed blissful ignorance and informing him, "Your father just sold all his possessions and paid a three thousand dollar fine for *your* lawlessness!" That is all he is told. No mention is made of the law or its demands.

Our speedster would probably answer, "So what? That was a silly thing for him to do," then drive off a little mystified but unmoved. Because of his ignorance of the law, the good news of his father's paying the fine makes no sense to him.

In the same way, because the sinner is ignorant of the *standard,* the *certainty,* and the *severity* of God's Law, the good news of the Father paying the penalty for him also makes no sense. He has no idea of what the Law demands of him—he doesn't understand the holiness of God. He doesn't realize the certainty of God's judgment—eternal damnation!

Because of this ignorance, the sinner continues in sin. He continues in the *"vanity of* [his] *mind, having the understanding darkened...through the ignorance that is in* [him], *because of the blindness of* [his] *heart"* (Ephesians 4:17–18 KJV). The good news of the Father's love in paying his penalty has no real meaning to him. Scripture truly states, *"The message of the cross is foolishness to those who are perishing"* (1 Corinthians 1:18).

Confronted by the Consequences

What will sober up our speedster? Suppose this time the policeman pulls him over but *does not mention any good news to him.* The officer informs him that thirty miles per hour is the maximum speed, manacles his wrists, and escorts him to court. After sentencing, he is taken to jail.

Only when he feels those steel handcuffs on his wrists, sees the severity of the sentence, and hears the prison door slam behind him is he in the right frame of mind to receive the good news! When he sees his true plight, he will no longer mock his father's way of escape. In fact, the *depth* to which our speedster sees his condition will determine his appreciation of the good news.

Can you see that the sinner must be confronted by the Law and all its consequences *before* he can appreciate the Father's paying the fine for him? Can you see that he needs to see the reality of the demands of the Law of God—that he must be led to a point of utter desperation before he can truly appreciate grace?

Proven Methods

John Wesley said, "Before I can preach love, mercy, and grace, I must preach sin, Law, and judgment." In writing to a young friend, he went so far as to advise, "Preach 90 percent Law and 10 percent grace."

Look at the way Charles Spurgeon, the "Prince of Preachers," used the Law of God to bring conviction.

> But more, there is war between you and God's Law. The Ten Commandments are against you. The first comes forward and says, "Let him be cursed, for he denies Me. He has another god besides Me, his god is his belly, he yieldeth homage to his lust." All the Ten Commandments, like ten great cannons, are pointed at you today, for you have broken all God's statutes, and lived in daily neglect of all His commands.
>
> Soul! you will find it a hard thing to go to war with the Law....What will you do when the Law comes in terror, when the trumpet of the archangel shall tear you from your grave, when the eyes of God shall burn their way into your guilty soul, when the great books shall be opened, and all your sin and shame shall be punished?

Can you imagine the desperation arising in the heart of a guilty sinner under such a fearful word? Only when he sees his depravity before his holy Creator and the severity of God's judgment will the cross make sense! Only then will he cry out in despair, "Woe is me, I'm undone!" or smite his breast with "God be merciful to me, a sinner!" The more he sees his guilt, the better.

The Bible says, *"Whoever calls on the name of the LORD shall be saved"* (Romans 10:13). With all his strength and

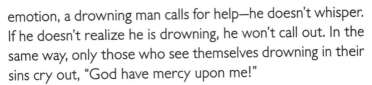

emotion, a drowning man calls for help—he doesn't whisper. If he doesn't realize he is drowning, he won't call out. In the same way, only those who see themselves drowning in their sins cry out, "God have mercy upon me!"

Spurgeon said, "They must be slain by the Law before they can be made alive by the Gospel!"

Look at these following relevant quotes from Charles Finney's book, *Revival Lectures.* (Keep in mind that Finney's ministry produced an 80 percent success rate!)

> It is of great importance that the sinner should be made to feel his guilt, and not left to the impression that he is unfortunate.

> Do not be afraid, but show him the breadth of the divine Law, and the exceeding strictness of its precepts. Make him see how it condemns his thoughts and life.

> By a convicted sinner, I mean *one who feels himself condemned by the Law of God,* as a guilty sinner. [italics added]

In other words, the sinner must see himself in truth. If our speedster hadn't seen his guilt, he would have sat in jail wondering, "What's wrong with a bit of drunk driving, anyway? I was only doing sixty miles per hour!" When the father arrived and said, "Son, I paid the fine for you," he would probably say, "About time, too, Dad. Now open this door—I wanna lay some rubber!"

On the other hand, what if his attitude had been one of brokenness? What if he had said, "What a fool I was. I could've killed someone—I deserve this!" When his father appeared at the prison door and told him he paid the fine for him anyway, the young man would be utterly broken by such a display of love and would live to honor his father.

The Purpose of the Law

The famous Spirit-filled evangelist, A. B. Earle, who wrote the hymns, "Bringing in the Sheaves," and "The Rest of Faith," supposedly preached more frequently than any other man living at the same time. In fifty years he traveled 325,000 miles in the United States and Canada, preached 19,780 times, and saw 150,000 persons converted in his meetings.

Earle was a strong believer in the preaching of future punishment. He said,

> I have found by long experience that the severest threatenings of the Law of God have a prominent place in leading men to Christ. They must see themselves lost before they will cry for mercy. They will not escape from danger until they see it.

The purpose of the Law is fourfold:

1. To show the world its *guilt* before God.
2. To give us the *knowledge* of sin.
3. To show us the *depth* of our sin.
4. To be a *schoolmaster* to lead us to Christ.

We have seen that ignorance of the Law leaves the sinner careless about his soul. The good news of Calvary is foolishness to him. The only way to awaken him is to show him the divine Law and all its consequences for the guilty soul. Then and only then will he be brought to a place of despair and cry out for salvation. No wonder the preaching of the Law is hell's best kept secret.

3

The Jesus Technique

I was once preaching on a street corner when a drunk began heckling me. His loud voice, however, was like music to my ears. He increased my crowd from about 20 to 150 people in a matter of minutes. Unfortunately, he didn't know when to stop—he wouldn't let me get a word in edgewise.

At one point, I got his attention and asked if he would like a sandwich. He declined, went back, sat in the front of the crowd, and continued to heckle me. Then he asked what kind of sandwiches they were. "Ham," I answered and held one out to him. As he took it and began eating, I started preaching.

After about ten seconds, he started heckling again. Pointing at him I yelled, "Don't talk with your mouth full!" The crowd roared, and he shut up.

Leaving People Speechless

There is a better way, however, to stop the clamor and questioning of sinners. Jesus knew how to do so. In fact, He was an expert at leaving people speechless. Let's look at a classic example.

> And behold, a certain lawyer stood up and tested
> Him, saying, "Teacher, what shall I do to inherit eter-
> nal life?" He said to him, "What is written in the
> law? What is your reading of it?" So he answered
> and said, "'You shall love the LORD your God with all
> your heart, with all your soul, with all your strength,
> and with all your mind,' and 'your neighbor as your-
> self.'" And He said to him, "You have answered
> rightly; do this and you will live." But he, wanting to
> justify himself, said to Jesus, "And who is my neigh-
> bor?"   (Luke 10:25–29)

When this man asked what he should do to inherit eternal life, Jesus did not give him the Good News—He pointed
to the Law. Look carefully at the result. *"But he, **wanting
to justify himself**, said to Jesus, 'And who is my neighbor?'"*
(Luke 10:29, emphasis added).

The Living Bible depicts the lawyer's attitude more
clearly. *"The man wanted to justify (his lack of love for some
kinds of people), so he asked, 'Which neighbors?'"* (Luke
10:29 TLB). When the lawyer became conscious of his guilt,
he sought to cover his sins. Why? Because the Law exposed
him!

Using the parable of the Good Samaritan, Jesus then
explained to the lawyer, an "expert" on the Law, what the
Law *actually* required. When the hero of the story turned
out to be a Samaritan, whom the Jews despised, the lawyer
was put in his place. After the parable, Jesus pointedly
asked,

> "So which of these three do you think was neighbor
> to him who fell among the thieves?" And he said,

"He who showed mercy on him." Then Jesus said to him, *"Go and do likewise."* (Luke 10:36–37)

What was the lawyer's surprising response? He was left speechless—without justification. There was no way he could justify himself—it was clear he was guilty!

Look at what D. L. Moody said about the importance of preaching the Law:

> God, being a perfect God, had to give a perfect Law, and the Law was given not to save men, but to measure them. I want you to understand this clearly, because I believe hundreds and thousands stumble at this point. They try to save themselves by trying to keep the Law; but it was never meant for men to save themselves by.
>
> Ask Paul why it was given. Here is his answer: *"That every mouth may be stopped, and all the world may become guilty before God"* (Romans 3:19). The Law stops every man's mouth. I can always tell a man who is near the kingdom of God; his mouth is stopped. This, then, is why God gives us the Law—to show us ourselves in our true colors. [quoted from *Select Sermons*]

No Excuse

Recently I discovered what it means to have my "mouth stopped." I was driving to a film developer that was located on a one-way street. Unfortunately, I took a wrong turn and found myself at the bottom of that street. Even though the store was only forty feet from the corner, I would have to go around the block to get to it—or would I? If I angled my car slightly to the left, I could be in their parking lot within two or three seconds—and that is precisely what I did!

As I turned the motor off, I noticed the law! A traffic officer had seen my little time saver. As he strolled across the street, my first reaction was to panic. Perhaps if I just ignore him, I thought, he will go away. I grabbed my negatives and ran into the film developer. At the counter I discovered I had grabbed the wrong envelope in my haste! Remembering my commitment to Christ, I determined in my heart to return and face the consequences.

I walked back to my car and said to the stern-looking traffic officer (who was patiently waiting), "I'm sorry, I did wrong." I sat in my car as he looked at my license.

"Have you any excuse for going the wrong way up a one-way street?" Different alibis flashed through my mind, but nothing seemed to justify my action. All I could think of was "guilty"!

I said, "No excuse whatsoever, officer."

My mouth was shut. I was totally exposed and therefore deserved whatever the law demanded. After a long pause, he said, "Well, there was no inconvenience to the traffic flow—and I don't think you will do it again." As he walked away I could see a twinkle in his eye.

That traffic officer had within his authority the discretion to judge whether or not I was truly sorry for my crime. How did he do that? By what came out of my mouth. I am sure that if I had offered any justification whatsoever he would have brought the full wrath of the law upon me.

But when my mouth was stopped, he could see I was truly penitent. He discerned my genuine sorrow and chose to show me leniency. In the same way, God made provision through the cross of Calvary to shower His mercy upon all who show godly sorrow for their transgression of the Law.

Washing with the Mirror?

Obviously, if we look into a mirror and see dirt on our face, we don't proceed to unhook the mirror and wash ourselves with it! No, we decide to use water because of what we have seen in the mirror.

The Law shows us our true state—that we are dirty before God. Washing ourselves with the Law is as foolish as cleansing our face with the mirror. The Law is the mirror that motivates us to be cleansed by the blood of Christ.

Notice that when Jesus answered the lawyer's question, He didn't preach the cross. Jesus did not say, *"Most assuredly, I say to you, unless one is born again, he cannot see the kingdom of God"* (John 3:3). He did not say, *"Believe on the Lord Jesus Christ, and you will be saved"* (Acts 16:31).

Why didn't Jesus preach the Good News to the lawyer? Scripture reveals the attitude of his heart. *"And behold, a certain lawyer stood up and **tested** Him, saying, 'Teacher, what shall I do to inherit eternal life?'"* (Luke 10:25, emphasis added).

Can you see that this man wasn't ready for the Good News? His question was not an inquiry of contrition. He wasn't repentant; he had no knowledge of sin because he had no understanding of the Law. The apostle Paul described such a person as *"being **ignorant** of God's righteousness, and seeking to establish their own righteousness"* (Romans 10:3, emphasis added).

Ready for Grace

On the Day of Pentecost, Peter preached to Jews who were devout men. *Eulabes,* the Greek word used for *devout,* literally means "taking hold well." In other words, the Jews grasped the meaning of the Law.

If you study that passage (Acts 2), you'll notice that Peter did not preach the Law. Why? He didn't need to—he just preached Christ crucified. As a result, these Jews cried out with repentant hearts for direction.

> *Now when they heard this, they* **were cut to the heart,** *and said to Peter and the rest of the apostles, "Men and brethren, what shall we do?"*
> (Acts 2:37–38, emphasis added)

The Law had been a schoolmaster to bring them to Christ.

Like the Jews gathered for Pentecost, Cornelius was a devout man. The Law of God upon his heart made him conscious of sin. Therefore, he didn't need more Law; he needed grace. As soon as Christ was preached, the Holy Spirit fell on all who heard Peter's words. (See Acts 10:44.)

Nicodemus, a ruler of the Jews, approached Jesus in a different spirit. He had not come to tempt Christ. He came with an understanding of the Law; he was guilty before God, and he knew it. He came with a humble acknowledgement of the divinity of Christ. Jesus pointed to the cross. He didn't need to mention the Law, sin, or judgment—He just gave him the Good News.

Let's examine the acceptance of Christ by Nathanael:

> *Philip found Nathanael and said to him, "We have found Him of whom Moses in the law, and also*

> the prophets, wrote; Jesus of Nazareth, the son of Joseph." And Nathanael said to him, "Can anything good come out of Nazareth?" Philip said to him, "Come and see." Jesus saw Nathanael coming toward Him, and said of him, "Behold, an Israelite indeed, in whom is no deceit!" Nathanael said to Him, "How do You know me?" Jesus answered and said to him, "Before Philip called you, when you were under the fig tree, I saw you." Nathanael answered and said to Him, "Rabbi, You are the Son of God! You are the King of Israel!" (John 1:45–49)

We can only surmise what Nathanael was thinking under the fig tree, but the words of Jesus give us a good clue: "Behold, an Israelite [he was brought up under the Law] indeed [not just in word—he obeyed the Law], in whom there is no deceit [he read the way of God in truth, and didn't twist the Law to suit his own sins as did the Pharisees]."

I believe that Nathanael labored under the burden and weight of his sin. That is why he so readily embraced the Savior. Scripture also says, "The Law and the prophets were until John. Since that time the kingdom of God has been preached, and everyone is pressing into it" (Luke 16:16).

What does Scripture mean by the statement "everyone is pressing into it"? It means that the Law was doing its job in Israel. Multitudes were laboring and burdened under the guilt of their sin, and multitudes flocked to John the Baptist to acknowledge their guilt.

Wisdom in Witnessing

Not long after I discovered "hell's best kept secret," I was in Australia for a series of meetings. One afternoon I decided to take a break from my preparations and go for a walk. Seeing a female hitchhiker, I approached her and struck up a conversation. I soon found myself saying, "Why don't you become a Christian? It's exciting! God will give you real love and joy within your heart." She turned to me and said, "I can get that in the world!"

Immediately I realized that I had become traditional in my witnessing. Instead of driving this woman to Christ by using the Law, I had tried to attract her to Christ by dangling the benefits of salvation before her eyes. I quickly changed my approach and said, "Yes, but the world can't give you righteousness, and that is what you're going to need on Judgment Day. God will judge you by the standard of His Law. You know the Ten Commandments."

Suddenly she came under conviction and began looking for a car to pick her up. We can witness ourselves into a corner with the man-centered Gospel. We have made happiness, rather than righteousness, the issue.

One Sunday I decided to preach the Law in our own church. I had read in Finney's books about the sinner "sighing" and "heaving." Sure enough, a young woman walked down the aisle and stood at the altar sighing and heaving her shoulders. She was obviously under heavy conviction. I had never seen anything like it before.

In the area of personal witnessing, we need to discern whether the person is a "Nicodemus" or a hardened "Pharisee." You don't need a lot of discernment to discover a person's attitude toward sin and judgment.

Ask for wisdom in witnessing—God has promised to give it to you. (See James 1:5.) If you're sharing your faith with someone who has no understanding of sin, use the Law to awaken him. If he is burdened by the guilt of his sin, he doesn't need awakening; he needs the Savior.

Study the different examples in Scripture. The woman at the well needed little convincing of her sin; she knew she had broken the seventh commandment by committing adultery. (See John 4:15–26.)

The Roman jailer knew the Law of God in his heart. When he cried out to be saved, it was not from the earthquake that had already passed. He cried out in humility to be saved from the wrath against his sin. It was then that the apostle Paul preached Christ to him.

We should follow the tested words of Charles Finney who said,

> If you have an *unconverted* sinner, *convict* him. If you have a *convicted* sinner, *convert* him.

If you discover a passenger who doesn't see the need to put on a parachute because he is happy eating the meal and watching the onboard movie, don't say, "Please put it on—it will be even better than the movie and the meal!"

No, that doesn't make sense! If you want him to put it on and keep it on, tell him about the jump. Say, "Well, if you want to end up spread all over some field, go ahead—it's your choice." Then he will put it on for the right reason.

When you see sinners who haven't put on the Lord Jesus Christ, don't tell them He will improve their lives. That generates a wrong motive. Tell them about the jump: that *"it is appointed for men to die once, but after this the judgment"* (Hebrews 9:27); that the fist of eternal justice will grind them to powder if they remain in sin; that unless they repent, they will perish!

How Should Sinners Come?

When Jesus spoke of entering the kingdom of God, He made the following statements:

> *Enter ye in at the strait gate: for wide is the gate, and broad is the way, that leadeth to destruction, and many there be which go in thereat: because **strait** is the gate, and **narrow** is the way, which leadeth unto life, and few there be that find it.*
> (Matthew 7:13–14 KJV, emphasis added)

> ***Strive** to enter in at the **strait** gate: for many, I say unto you, will seek to enter in, and shall not be able.*
> (Luke 13:24 KJV, emphasis added)

A closer look at those original Greek words sheds some interesting light on how sinners should come before a holy God.

1. Strive—*agonizomai*, from which we derive the word *agonize.*
2. Narrow—*thlibo*, which means "to suffer affliction."
3. Strait—*stenos*, which means "groaning."

As with natural birth, intense agony, affliction, and groaning should accompany one's entrance into the kingdom of God. Joy and gladness are a *result* of the new birth, not *the way* in which one enters the kingdom of God.

Job stopped his continual attempts to justify himself when God gave His viewpoint. Job said, *"Behold, I am vile; what shall I answer You? I lay my hand over my mouth"* (Job 40:4).

As long as we use man's methods, sinners will continually justify their unlawful deeds. But when we use the Law, we are giving God's viewpoint, and that stops their mouths.

Often the man-centered Gospel is referred to as "easy believism." "Hard believism," or preaching a call to commitment, cross-bearing, self-denial, and holiness, must be accompanied by the Law of God. Otherwise your hearers will still lack the knowledge of sin. Law must precede grace.

Wherever Christ was preached in Scripture, the crowds consisted of Jews—those who knew the Law—or those who feared God and worked righteousness. But where the Gospel was preached to the ungodly, it was always preceded by the Law.

Do we think we know a better way? The ineffectiveness of our modern evangelical methods suggests that we must return to searching the Scriptures for a biblical way to share our faith.

4

Pushing for Commitment?

S ome time ago, a woman came to me in tears and
related how, two years previous, she and her husband
had heard the preaching of the Gospel. She had come
under tremendous conviction, taken hold of her husband's
hand, and pulled him up to the altar. Both had made a commitment to Christ.

She came to Christ because she saw her sin and knew
she needed mercy and forgiveness; he came to Christ to
please his wife. Although she was able to prop up her husband for two or three months, he eventually became lukewarm, then a backslider, then bitter. Now the marriage had
broken up, and she felt responsible.

I found it rather difficult to console her because she was
right—she was responsible. She was sincere but misguided.
He had turned from the holy commandment, and now the
"latter end is worse for them than the beginning" (2 Peter
2:20).

When I warn others about leading sinners to a commitment without any consciousness of sin, I speak from experience. As a new Christian in misguided zeal, with the "Four
Easy Steps" type of booklet in hand, I led twenty to thirty

people in the sinner's prayer. Unfortunately, 95 percent of them backslid.

I can see now that, although I was sincere, those I led in prayer were not crying out for mercy—they were just "giving this thing a try to see if it is as good as Ray says it is." My new "converts" were soon disillusioned. The following letter sums up the experience of many Christians who are equally disillusioned with modern evangelical methods:

> My friend and I have knocked on approximately 500 doors with the gospel message, and I have been utterly frustrated by the lack of response. Now we see how futile it is when the Law of God is excluded.
> We got a few "decisions," but nothing ever came of them. People often make decisions to get you off their back, and then make it impossible for you to get hold of them again.

Wisdom for Soulwinning

The Scriptures tell us, *"He who wins souls is wise"* (Proverbs 11:30). Needless to say, he who inoculates defeats the very purpose of evangelism. But the question arises—Is he wise because he wins souls, or does he win souls because he is wise?

If we are wise, we will discern the condition of a person's heart. Is he a sincere Nicodemus, or is he an arrogant lawyer who has no understanding of sin, righteousness, and judgment? If he is a Nicodemus, tell him the Good News; if he is a lawyer, use the Law to stir his conscience and will. If he is not conscious of his sin, bring conviction; if he is under conviction, convert him.

When the harvest is ripe, the fruit should practically fall into the basket. Think of the conversion of the Ethiopian eunuch. God led Philip to a soul that was ripe for salvation! If you have to twist and pull an apple off a branch, you will probably find it to be sour.

Jesus never pushed for a commitment from those who were not willing to forsake all. When the lawyer tested him with, *"What shall I do to inherit eternal life?"* (Luke 10:25), Jesus did not lead him in a sinner's prayer. He preached the Law to stir the sinner's conscience.

When many disciples turned back in John chapter six, Jesus did not compromise His doctrine to keep them in the kingdom. When Jesus told the rich young ruler to sell his goods, and he went away sorrowful, Jesus didn't call after him, "What about *half* your goods?"

I have been in large meetings where ministers preach the "Good News," emphasizing grace without Law, and then invite sinners to come to Jesus. The music begins to play gently, and a dozen counselors quietly walk to the altar to make a response easier for the sinner. On inquiry, I found that justification for such a method was "we will do anything to get people 'saved.'"

I'm not questioning the sincerity of those concerned, but I am looking at the fruit of the method. Perhaps one in ten sinners makes a genuine commitment, but what about the other nine who have been seduced into an emotional response? They have been inoculated against Christianity! I'm sure you will agree that some of the most difficult people to witness to are those who have at one time made a commitment and have grown cold or bitter toward the Gospel.

We have forgotten that God calls us to sow the seed and leave the results with Him. If we do reap with rejoicing, more than likely someone else has sown in tears. If we faithfully sow the seed, a lack of response is no reason to feel the burden of failure. Ministers need not prolong an altar call by having the congregation sing "Amazing Grace" twice more until a hand is raised. God is faithful—His Word cannot return void.

Hitting the Target

The good-soil hearer who bore fruit first heard the Word and understood it. We must make certain that the sinner hears the Word and that he understands the Word. He must not come to Christ still seeing the cross as foolishness; he must see it as the power of God.

The preacher must realize that it's not the "bang of the gun" that counts, but that the bullet hits the target. Some of us are concerned only about the delivery and not the object to which it is being delivered. The sinner must understand his sin, his depravity, his doom, and his judgment—and only the Law of God can effectively do that.

Nineteenth century evangelists skillfully wielded the Law of God in preaching—and reaped the fruit of true conversions. Remember these two important statements from preachers whose ministries were effective:

> This, then, is what God gives us the Law for—to show us ourselves in our true color.   —D. L. Moody

> I remark that [the Law] is the rule and the only just rule by which the guilt of sin can be measured.
> —Charles Finney

The good-soil hearer sees his true condition before the Judge of the universe. He cries from his heart of hearts, *"Woe is me, for I am undone!"* (Isaiah 6:5) and admits his wickedness. He receives the implanted Word in a good and honest heart and cries, *"Create in me a clean heart, O God"* (Psalm 51:10). His repentance and faith in God establish him on a sure foundation. He then brings forth fruit with patience. (See Luke 8:15.)

In quiet humility this new convert sends his roots deep into God's Word. He grows in faithfulness, in confession of sin, and in obedience to the Word as it unfolds to him.

When the Going Gets Tough

Because of his fertile soil and deep roots, our good-soil hearer can only benefit from the sunlight. When persecution, tribulation, and temptation come, they only cause him to grow. Trials send his roots even deeper in search of moisture. Not only will he bring forth good fruit, but his fruit will remain. (See John 15:16.)

Just as our friend put his parachute on for the jump and not for a happy flight, so our good-soil hearer came to the cross for the right reason. He rejoices in tribulation because his name is written in heaven. The flight may be rough, but he is safe as long as he keeps his parachute firmly upon his back.

The apostle Paul and Silas were having a rough flight after receiving many lashes and being cast into prison. Instead of being trapped in self-pity, they prayed and sang praises to God. (See Acts 16:25.) They weren't rejoicing about the flight; they were rejoicing because their names were written in heaven. When the heat of tribulation burned down upon them, they didn't wither and die—they grew!

With this thought in mind, what else does Scripture say about tribulation? *"My brethren, count it all joy when you fall into various trials, knowing that the testing of your faith produces patience"* (James 1:2–3).

In other words, little plant, be joyful when the sun shines upon you, because it will bring forth the fruit of patience. The apostle Paul also saw the benefit of sunlight: *"I am exceedingly joyful in all our tribulation"* (2 Corinthians 7:4).

Scripture also says, *"In this you greatly rejoice, though now for a little while, if need be, you have been grieved by various trials"* (1 Peter 1:6). In other words, "Little plant, you may droop slightly at first as the heat of the sun begins to burn upon your leaves, but it is only *'if need be.'"*

Because He is a loving and caring husbandman, God makes sure that the plant gets just enough sunlight. He knows that sunlight will cause its roots to extend in search of moisture. Often a tree's roots go deeper than its height and extend further than the branches. Some large trees draw as much as 250 gallons of water from the soil daily! The roots of a tree always grow toward the moisture.

The genuine saint will always grow toward the Spirit of God in tribulation. The sunlight will drive him to his knees in humble surrender. He will not clench his fist at God at the first sign of problems.

Affliction Works for Us

In retrospect, my greatest time of yielding to God was during my wilderness experience—just after my conversion.

I had never known such a heaviness, but it drove me to my knees in search of moisture. Often we blame tribulation on the enemy when God uses this very instrument to fulfill His will for our lives.

The Holy Spirit led Jesus into His wilderness experience. (See Luke 4:1.) Though He was a Son, He learned obedience by the things He suffered. Psalm 66 shows us why we should not despise the heat of tribulation:

> *Oh, bless our God, you peoples! And make the voice of His praise to be heard, who keeps our soul among the living, and does not allow our feet to be moved. For You, O God, have tested us; You have refined us as silver is refined. You brought us into the net; You laid affliction on our backs. You have caused men to ride over our heads; we went through fire and through water; but You brought us out to rich fulfillment.* (Psalm 66:8–12)

God takes us through the fire, not to burn us, but to purify us. He takes us through the water, not to drown us, but to wash us. Understanding that the Lord chastens those He loves enables us to endure trials. *"Our light affliction, which is but for a moment, is working for us a far more exceeding and eternal weight of glory"* (2 Corinthians 4:17).

Can you see that affliction works for us? My time of trial in my wilderness experience worked for me. God demonstrated His purpose, so that I might grow and bring forth fruit. David said, *"It is good for me that I have been afflicted, that I may learn Your statutes"* (Psalm 119:71). One who is soundly saved will grow spiritually during trials and temptations. That is one evidence of genuine repentance and true salvation.

Looking for Fruit

There's another way to determine the condition of a convert's soul. Scripture exhorts us to examine ourselves to see if we *"are in the faith"* (2 Corinthians 13:5). Should we search out our decision card or check the church membership? No, we are to search for fruit.

For the sake of our fellowship and for the sake of the sinner, we need to evaluate our new converts and look for fruit. Why? First, to mark those who cause division and to look out for wolves among the sheep:

> *Beware of false prophets, who come to you in sheep's clothing, but inwardly they are ravenous wolves. You will know them by their fruits.*
> (Matthew 7:15–16)

> *For I know this, that after my departure savage wolves will come in among you, not sparing the flock. Also from among yourselves men shall rise up, speaking perverse things, to draw away the disciples after themselves.* (Acts 20:29–30)

> *They went out from us, but they were not of us; for if they had been of us, they would have continued with us; but they went out that they might be made manifest, that none of them were of us.*
> (1 John 2:19)

A gospel that draws sinners to a commitment without a consciousness of sin will produce a harvest of those who have no zeal, fire, or fruit—they are not "hot" for God.

Fruitless, lukewarm Christians are not truly part of Christ's body—they merely weigh heavy in His stomach until

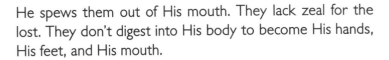

He spews them out of His mouth. They lack zeal for the lost. They don't digest into His body to become His hands, His feet, and His mouth.

Fruit That Remains

In a book called *Evangelism as a Lifestyle,* Jim Petersen, an experienced evangelist, shares his concerns about superficial conversions. He writes about many mass evangelical crusades having a tremendous effect on Christendom...for about three months!

Petersen makes this sobering statement:

> Saturation evangelism crusades have been carried out on numerous occasions in Latin America and in our countries. But studies done on their effectiveness by various missiologists show *little or no lasting growth.*

In a chapter called "The Heritage Factor," he looks at the "meager results of the apostle Paul's preaching to a pagan crowd (Acts 17:34) and the amazing results of Peter's preaching at Pentecost (Acts 2:37–41)." He continues:

> What was the difference? Was Peter more Spirit-filled? Was Peter a better communicator? No. The difference was that the Jews' religious heritage prepared them to respond eagerly to the Gospel.

How close the author is to the truth—it was the Law, which was a schoolmaster that brought them to Christ!

Many men of God are frustrated because of what they see in the church today. Generally speaking, we are not the mighty army we should be. Our churches are full of stony-ground hearers who are tares among the wheat, murmurers, complainers, quenchers of the Spirit, and wolves among the sheep. They *look* as if they are entering into the sheepfold by the door, but in truth they climb up some other way, and our sincere twenty-first century evangelical methods are accommodating them!

We need to return to the basics of biblical evangelism and, where necessary, use the Law to bring the knowledge of sin. Only then we will see wasted, unregenerate lives transformed into fervent, effective, faithful, and fiery laborers who will turn their world right side up for the kingdom of God!

5

The Forgotten Key

I once spoke with a man who was mystified as to why people cross the white line of morality. "On one side of the white line you have law-abiding citizens who pay their taxes and are generally good people," he asserted. "On the other side of the line you have those who are lawless and corrupt. What makes people cross the white line?"

I told him that the "white line" was there because he had put it there; on one side was his idea of good, and the other side his idea of evil. The Law, God's "white line," is ten miles up the street!

Man deceives himself by making God in his own image. God rebuked His own people, saying, *"You thought that I was altogether like you"* (Psalm 50:21). In other words, man thinks that God shares his moral standards; but Jesus told the Pharisees, *"What is highly esteemed among men is an abomination in the sight of God"* (Luke 16:15).

We find consolation by comparing ourselves to human standards. When we take a look at the rest of humanity, none of us fares too badly. *"But they, measuring themselves by themselves, and comparing themselves among themselves, are not wise"* (2 Corinthians 10:12).

Written on Our Hearts

The only standard with which people should compare themselves is the Law of God. Most evangelicals, however, shy away from even mentioning the Law in preaching or in personal witnessing. Why is this? Probably because they are ignorant of its true function. They are mystified by Scriptures such as, *"The law of the LORD is perfect, converting the soul"* (Psalm 19:7).

Scripture tells us that even Gentiles, who were not raised under the Law,

> show the work of the law written in their hearts, their conscience also bearing witness, and between themselves their thoughts accusing or else excusing them. (Romans 2:15)

In other words, God's Law is written on the heart of every man. The most primitive tribes in deepest Africa have God's Law written on their hearts—they know "Thou shalt not kill," "Thou shalt not steal," "Thou shalt not commit adultery." When we use the Law to convict Jews or Gentiles, it confirms what man already knows within his heart.

Charles Finney, speaking of the use of the Law to expose sin, said,

> I remark that this is the rule, *and the only just rule* by which the guilt of sin can be measured...every man need only consult his own consciousness faithfully and he will see that it is equally affirmed by the mind's own intuition to be right. [from *The Guilt of Sin,* italics added]

If we are serious about reaching this world for God, we must return to the biblical principle of evangelism and use the Law of God.

The Law Convicts of Sin

When Jesus stood up to read in the synagogue on the Sabbath, He quoted the following Old Testament passage:

> *The Spirit of the Lord GOD is upon me; because the LORD hath anointed me to preach good tidings unto the meek; he hath sent me to bind up the brokenhearted, to proclaim liberty to the captives, and the opening of the prison to them that are bound;...to give unto them beauty for ashes, the oil of joy for mourning, the garment of praise for the spirit of heaviness.* (Isaiah 61:1, 3 KJV)

This portion of Scripture reveals to whom Christ was anointed to preach the Gospel. Jesus came to the *"meek,"* the *"brokenhearted,"* the *"captives,"* the *"bound,"* to those who mourn, and to those who are in *"heaviness."* What a perfect description of the guilty sinner!

The convicted sinner mourns because of his transgressions; he sees himself as a prisoner of sin; his heart is broken and heavy before God—not with the problems of daily living, but with the guilt of sin. The "glad tidings" are foolishness to the unawakened sinner, but to the awakened sinner they are indeed welcome words.

In the Sermon on the Mount, Jesus said that the poor in spirit, those who mourn, and those who are meek are *"blessed"* (Matthew 5:3–5). Why? Because their condition enables them to receive the Gospel as the power of God unto salvation.

The unawakened sinner is not mourning, poor, or meek and, therefore, needs the Law to bring the knowledge of sin. Until then, he feels the preaching of the cross is foolishness.

Governor Felix was such an unawakened sinner until the apostle Paul had the opportunity to speak with him.

> And after some days, when Felix came with his wife Drusilla, who was Jewish, he sent for Paul and heard him concerning the faith in Christ. Now as he reasoned about righteousness, self-control, and the judgment to come, Felix was afraid and answered, "Go away for now; when I have a convenient time I will call for you."   (Acts 24:24–25)

The apostle Paul did not preach the cross; he just talked of sin, righteousness, and judgment. Obviously, Paul mentioned the righteousness that is of the Law and judgment by the Law because *"Felix trembled"* (v. 25 KJV). Paul put his finger on Felix's sin—his god was his belly! He had broken the first commandment.

Jesus said, *"And when He* [the Holy Spirit] *has come, He will convict the world of sin, and of righteousness, and of judgment"* (John 16:8). Once Governor Felix was confronted with his sin, the ball was in his court. Scripture, however, is silent on his decision.

The Law Produces Understanding

Melanchthon, a German scholar and religious reformer, admonished that the Ten Commandments be diligently preached so that the people might learn to fear God and be moved to genuine repentance.

> You understand that the work of the Law is the revealing of sin. Furthermore, when I speak of sin, I include all kinds of sin—external, internal, hypocrisy, unbelief, love of self, and contempt for or ignorance of God—which are certainly the very roots of all human

works. In the justification of sinners the first work of God is to reveal our sin; to confound our conscience, make us tremble, terrify us, briefly, to condemn us...

The beginning of repentance consists of that work of the Law by which the Spirit of God terrifies and confounds consciences....Just as the Christian life must certainly begin with the knowledge of sin, so Christian doctrine must begin with the function of the Law.

The unawakened sinner will not seek God until he understands his true condition before his Creator. *"There is none who understands; there is none who seeks after God"* (Romans 3:11). As we will see from Scripture, the evangelist must bring about this understanding through preaching and teaching.

God wants sinners to be taught. *"Good and upright is the LORD; therefore He **teaches** sinners in the way"* (Psalm 25:8, emphasis added). After David cried out for a clean heart before God, he said, *"Then I will **teach** transgressors Your ways, and sinners shall be converted to You"* (Psalm 51:13, emphasis added).

Your hearers must understand before they can respond to the Gospel. The good-soil hearer was *"he who hears the word and **understands** it"* (Matthew 13:23, emphasis added).

Jesus said, *"Go ye therefore, and **teach** all nations...**teaching** them to observe all things whatsoever I have commanded you"* (Matthew 28:19–20 KJV, emphasis added). The disciples were obedient to that commission:

> Daily in the temple, and in every house, they did not cease **teaching** and preaching Jesus as the Christ.
> (Acts 5:42, emphasis added)

> *A servant of the Lord must not quarrel but be gentle to all, **able to teach,** patient, in humility **correcting** those who are in opposition.*
> (2 Timothy 2:24–25, emphasis added)

In perhaps the most frequently quoted passage of Hosea, God lamented, *"My people are destroyed for **lack of knowledge**"* (Hosea 4:6, emphasis added).

Many have separated preaching from teaching, somehow thinking that the cross of Christ is such a mystery that understanding comes *solely* by illumination of the Holy Spirit. Obviously, there is no salvation if God doesn't grant repentance and draw sinners to Himself, but He has committed to His people the word of reconciliation.

By God's grace we can produce understanding and, using God's methods, work with Him to see conviction and repentance. Remember what Philip asked the Ethiopian eunuch: *"Do you **understand** what you are reading?"* (Acts 8:30, emphasis added.) Philip, the evangelist, took time to teach.

The Law Builds Faith

Often when we are preaching we don't realize that we should be watering as well as sowing. We should be preaching *and* teaching. Others have sown in the sinner's heart, and his level of understanding is further on than those who are hearing the Word for the first time. His understanding may be darkened, but every principle taught by the evangelist, which the sinner understands, produces more light within his heart.

In an article entitled "How to Preach without Results," Charles Finney said, "Preach salvation by grace; but ignore the condemned and lost condition of the sinner, lest he should understand what you mean by grace, and feel his need of it."

Any portion of Scripture that we teach the sinner will not only give him more light, but it will also produce faith in his heart. As he grasps a story of faith, obedience, or love, he is not just hearing a story of a woman with an issue of blood, but he is hearing the Word of God, and *"faith comes by hearing, and hearing by the word of God"* (Romans 10:17).

Remember, they will flee from the wrath to come only if they believe that there is wrath to come. *"But the word preached did not profit them, not being mixed with faith in them that heard it"* (Hebrews 4:2 KJV).

We can begin a sermon on any portion of Scripture, knowing that this is no ordinary book—it is God's Word. We are not just relating a Bible incident to fill in time until we preach Scriptures that bring conviction. We are also laying a foundation of understanding and faith within the heart. As the sinner hears the Word and understands it, faith will rise in his heart. This prepares the way for the evangelist to proclaim the weightier matters of the Law, bring conviction, and thus cause the sinner to thirst after grace.

The Law Exposes Sin

In my own unsaved condition, I had a sense of security in my ignorance of the Law. My attitude was, "I will probably get to heaven, if there is one, because I haven't broken any of the Ten Commandments—whatever they are." I admitted to knowing four of the commandments:

1. Thou shalt not steal.

59

2. Thou shalt not lie.
3. Thou shalt not murder.
4. Thou shalt not commit adultery.

Here was my justification:

1. My stealing was limited to raiding apple orchards, which doesn't really count.
2. Any lies I may have told were only "petty."
3. I hadn't murdered anyone.
4. I hadn't committed adultery.

Because my infractions were only minor, I concluded that I would probably make it. Rather pathetic, isn't it? But it is so common!

I remained willfully ignorant of the truth. Not once did I open the Bible to see what the other six commandments had to say—I didn't dare! I was a happy sinner who was enjoying the pleasures of sin for a season. I had no burden of guilt until I read this passage on the night of my conversion:

> You have heard that it was said to those of old, "You shall not commit adultery." But I say to you that whoever looks at a woman to lust for her has already committed adultery with her in his heart.
> (Matthew 5:27–28)

Jesus brought that seventh commandment to its true light. Immediately I saw that God's standard was unattainable. I had transgressed the seventh commandment a multitude of times. I had not resisted lust; I had run to it, embraced it, and taken pleasure in it. I had loved darkness much more than light.

The Law on my heart cried out, "Guilty, guilty!" My conscience screamed, "Yes, yes, the Law of God is true—guilty,

guilty, guilty!" I had no words of justification; my mouth was completely stopped! That night I called upon the Lord as a dying man and embraced the Good News that Jesus had suffered my punishment.

What actually happened to me? I came to the knowledge of my sin by the Law in the light of New Testament revelation. The quick and powerful words of Christ tore away my pathetic self-deception.

In John Bunyan's spiritual autobiography, *Grace Abounding to the Chief of Sinners,* he shared his conversion experience:

> Something else happened that I have often thought of with thanksgiving. When I was a soldier, I was sent with some others to a certain plain to besiege it; but just as I was ready to go, someone asked to go in my place, and as he stood sentry duty, he was shot in the head with a musket bullet and died.
>
> These, as I have said, were some of God's judgments and mercies. *But none of these things awakened my soul to righteousness,* so I kept on sinning and grew more and more rebellious against God and careless of my own salvation....I never considered that sin would damn me, no matter what religion I followed, unless I was found in Christ....
>
> But one day it happened that, among the various sermons our parson preached, his subject was "The Sabbath Day" and the evil of breaking it either with work or sports or in any other way. Then my conscience began to prick me, and I thought that he had preached this sermon on purpose to show me my evil ways. That was the first time I can remember that I felt guilty and very burdened, for the moment at least,

and I went home when the sermon was ended with a great depression upon my spirit.

Can you see that consciousness of sin came to Bunyan when he realized that he had broken the fourth commandment? Despite God's mercy in sparing his life, Bunyan didn't come to Christ until he heard the Law preached.

The Law Prepares the Sinner

John Bunyan's conversion and my own experience demonstrate that the Law of God prepares a sinner to receive the grace of God. Can this principle be supported in the Scriptures? Let's examine a New Testament passage to find out.

Zacchaeus, a chief tax collector who had profited by extorting his fellow Jews, climbed a tree to see Jesus as He passed through the streets of Jericho. What happened when this shrewd moneymaker encountered Christ?

And when Jesus came to the place, He looked up and saw him, and said to him, "Zacchaeus, make haste and come down, for today I must stay at your house." So he made haste and came down, and received Him joyfully. But when they saw it, they all complained, saying, "He has gone to be a guest with a man who is a sinner." Then Zacchaeus stood and said to the Lord, "Look, Lord, I give half of my goods to the poor; and if I have taken anything from anyone by false accusation, I restore fourfold." And Jesus said unto him, "Today salvation has come to this house, because he also is a son of Abraham; for the Son of Man has come to seek and to save that which was lost." (Luke 19:5–10)

What motivated Zacchaeus' conversion? Bringing a hard-ened sinner to salvation obviously requires more than curi-osity. Zacchaeus' decision to restore fourfold shows that he knew the Law. *"If a man steals...a sheep...he shall restore... four sheep for a sheep"* (Exodus 22:1). The Law brought the knowledge of sin, resulting in genuine repentance and salva-tion.

Look at what Bible teacher Paris Reidbead says:

> When one hundred years ago earnest scholars decreed that the Law had no relationship to the preaching of the Gospel, they deprived the Holy Spirit in the area where their influence prevailed of the only instrument with which He had ever armed Himself to prepare sinners for grace.

The Law Is the Schoolmaster

When a scribe told Jesus the demands of the Law, Jesus said, *"You are not far from the kingdom of God"* (Mark 12:34). In other words, the Law was acting as a "school-master." That same verse reports, *"But after that no one dared question Him."* Why? Because the Law "stops the mouth."

When the apostle Paul spoke to hardhearted Jews,

> *he explained and solemnly testified of the kingdom of God, persuading them concerning Jesus from both the **Law of Moses** and the Prophets, from morning till evening.* (Acts 28:23, emphasis added)

Paul used the Law as an evangelical tool to reach the lost. *"Knowing this, that the law is not made for a righteous man, but...for sinners"* (1 Timothy 1:9 KJV).

Jesus strongly reproved the lawyers (teachers of the Law) with the following rebuke:

> Woe to you lawyers! **For you have taken away the key of knowledge.** You did not enter in yourselves, and those who were entering in you hindered.
>
> (Luke 11:52, emphasis added)

They had failed to teach the Law in truth. The Law is the key of knowledge. With the Law comes the knowledge of sin; the Law acts as a schoolmaster to teach sinners in the way. So often we hear *"My people are destroyed for lack of knowledge"* (Hosea 4:6). What knowledge did they lack? In that same verse God said to His people, *"You have forgotten the law of your God."*

The apostle Paul affirmed, *"I had not known sin, but by the law"* (Romans 7:7 KJV). How can a sinner repent if he doesn't know what sin is? And if he doesn't repent, he will perish. (See Luke 13:3.) Lack of knowledge destroys the sinner. The Law is the key that unlocks the door to the Savior; it is the schoolmaster to bring men and women to Christ.

Changing Our Approach

If using the Law cuts against the grain of your evangelical methods, may I encourage you to be open and pray about it? In recent years I have changed my whole approach to preaching and personal witnessing.

As I began to grasp the use of the Law, I was like a child with a new toy. I couldn't wait for an opportunity to try it out on some unsuspecting sinner. At the time, I was with my family on a long weekend holiday.

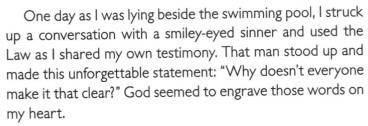

One day as I was lying beside the swimming pool, I struck up a conversation with a smiley-eyed sinner and used the Law as I shared my own testimony. That man stood up and made this unforgettable statement: "Why doesn't everyone make it that clear?" God seemed to engrave those words on my heart.

If you grasp the principle of using the Law to bring conviction, please ask the Lord for great wisdom. (See James 3:17.) Most of our fellow believers can see the Law only in the light of justification. They don't realize that *"the Law is good, if anyone uses it lawfully [for the purpose for which it was designed]"* (1 Timothy 1:8 AMP).

The minute you mention the Law, most Christians will probably encourage you to read Paul's epistle to the legalistic Galatians. More than likely you will be misunderstood by those who preach only grace. You may even seem harsh and unloving in your delivery. You may be accused of trying to condemn the sinner.

An elderly, sincere Christian once tapped me on the arm while I was preaching outdoors. He gently said, "I feel condemned, brother," and left. Unfortunately, I was only three-quarters of the way through my delivery. I'm sure Wesley was misunderstood with his "90 percent Law and 10 percent grace."

Melanchthon, the man largely responsible for Luther's understanding of grace, said:

> But there are many who speak only of the forgiveness of sin, but who say little or nothing about repentance. If there is nevertheless no forgiveness of sins without repentance, so also forgiveness of sins cannot be understood without repentance. Therefore, if

forgiveness of sins is preached without repentance, it follows that the people imagine they have already received the forgiveness of sins, and thereby they become cocksure and fearless, which is then greater error and sin than all the error that preceded our time.

Some believers may say, "I don't need all this Law business to get decisions. My message is, 'Turn or Burn!'" Well, preach hell without the Law and you will get decisions, but those who come will come in fear, rather than repentance. They will come to escape the fires of hell, and deep in their minds, they will think that God is unjust. Without knowledge of the Law, they will fail to see that they deserved hell. Consequently they will lack gratitude, the prime motivation for evangelism. The Law shows the sinner that he deserves hell; that's its purpose. There are no shortcuts.

Recently I spoke to a respected man of God who shared with me his frustration in reaping only lukewarm commitments. His frustration had led him to a point of interrogating sinners at the altar to see if they meant their commitment.

Brethren, the fault isn't with the sinner; he's just responding to the message as he understands it. We need to change our approach and bring heartfelt conviction by using the Law.

6

No Anointing—No Results

One day while I was typing in my office, I spied a daddy longlegs sitting on the red carpet. Disgusted that a spider had the nerve to distract me from my work, I stopped typing, picked up the little critter, and tossed it out the door.

Five minutes later I glanced to my right and was astounded that another spider had made its way to the same spot. I carefully stalked the creature, picked it up by its legs, and tossed it out the door. Sitting at my desk only minutes later, I caught a sight I could not believe—another spider of the same kind had made its way to the same spot!

Indignation consumed me! I stomped across, bent down, and was surprised by the most pathetic sight I had ever seen in my whole life. There lay one daddy longlegs with only three legs left. I had been throwing legs—not spiders—out the door!

Nothing is as helpless as a daddy longlegs with only three legs. The poor creature just limped around in circles. A worm has more defense than a writhing, dismembered spider. I didn't know what to do, so I placed it in the yard and tried to forget what I had done.

As an unbeliever, I was like that spider, crawling around in circles of futility with no means of defense or escape. I was without God, without Christ, without hope, without understanding, in the blackness of my ignorance, tormented by the fear of death.

The young man who led me to Christ could not believe that I had gotten saved. Throughout the next day he kept mumbling, "Ray Comfort—a Christian. I can't believe it!" He found my conversion difficult to believe because I had appeared so self-sufficient.

I can understand how he had gained such an impression. I had everything in life that anyone could ever want, yet he could not see that on the inside I was screaming! Everything I possessed was going to be snatched from me. Everything I loved was going to be torn from my hands. I could see that death's insatiable appetite was waiting to feed on me. Had my friend known the true condition of my life, he wouldn't have been surprised that I fled to Christ for mercy!

If you have never been tormented by the terrors of death, you may lack one very powerful motivating force for evangelism. Knowing that there are multitudes who are going through the very real horror of that impending appointment, I am driven to reach the lost. If any of them are going through even half of what I went through before the mercy of God reached down to me, God help them.

A Herd of Elephants?

In John chapter four, Jesus left Judea and departed again into Galilee. Then the Scriptures tell us that He *"must needs go through Samaria"* (v. 4 KJV). A dictionary reveals four definitions for the word *must.*

1. new wine
2. mold
3. a herd of stampeding male elephants
4. to be obligated

Obviously, the Scriptures refer to the fourth meaning; yet all four could justifiably be directed at the contemporary church. I pray that the new wine of the Holy Spirit would cause this moldy church to arise and become a herd of stampeding male elephants for the kingdom of God!

Jesus *must* go through Samaria to keep a divine appointment. The Father's one hand was guiding the Son, while His other guided the woman of Samaria. Jesus could do nothing of Himself. His testimony was, *"I must work the works of Him who sent Me"* (John 9:4). His burden was for the lost sinners who blindly walked through the darkness of this world. Obligation consumed Him. He *must* be about His Father's business—He *must* preach the kingdom of God!

We, too, *must* go through Samaria. We *must* be about our Father's business!

The Last Generation

Far too many of us have the name *Christian* yet fail to follow in the footsteps of Jesus. We love our holy huddles and Christian cliques. We have lost sight of the world with all its pains. The world is our Samaria. If we don't pass through it, how are we going to reach hell-bound sinners? Too often we don't see that separation from sin and separation from sinners are two completely different things!

I am not alone in thinking this is the last generation before the coming of Christ. In this generation, more than any other, men are *"lovers of themselves, lovers of money, boasters, proud, blasphemers, disobedient to parents, unthankful, unholy"* (2 Timothy 3:2). This conviction was reinforced by an article I read recently in a Christian newspaper.

According to *Gabler's Research Newsletter,* the problems in schools in the United States in 1940 were: talking, chewing gum, making noise, running in halls, getting out of line, wearing improper clothing, and not putting paper in the wastepaper baskets.

Look at the major problems reported in recent years: rape, robbery, assault, burglary, arson, bombings, murder, suicide, absenteeism, vandalism, extortion, drug-pushing, drug abuse, alcohol abuse, gang warfare, pregnancies, abortions, and venereal disease. No doubt you can add to the list today. We have a tremendous obligation to this generation.

As if these problems aren't bad enough, death itself is unleashing its fury against thousands of souls each day. With such obvious needs surrounding us, have we lost our ability to fight against an insidious enemy who ensnares our loved ones, coworkers, and friends by deceit and deception?

Too Close to the Soul

A very interesting portion of Scripture addresses this issue. When Nahash the Ammonite encamped against Jabesh-Gilead, the men of Jabesh sought a covenant with Nahash. What were the demands of such an agreement? Nahash said, *"On this condition will I make a covenant with you, that I may thrust out all your right eyes, and lay it for a reproach upon all Israel"* (1 Samuel 11:2 KJV).

By consulting a Bible dictionary, I discovered that the name *Nahash* means "serpent," leaving no doubt that this is a type of that old serpent, the devil, seeking a covenant with the church.

Nahash actually had a method to his madness. Warriors in those days fought with the left side covered with a shield, making the right eye the fighting eye. Nahash was seeking to destroy Jabesh's ability to fight.

Can you imagine actually being there? How would you have reacted after hearing the demands of the covenant? Would you have said, "So Nahash wants to thrust out our right eyes. Well, I want some details before I make any decision. Does he want to gouge them out with his finger, scrape them out with a knife, or use the old red-hot poker? Before I make any decisions, I want details"?

No sane person would react in such a way. No one would ever consider having someone thrust out his eye. I'd rather lose a thousand ears; but an eye—that's too close to the soul! The immediate pain and the resulting darkness make such a thought odious.

In the same way, the very thought of the body of Christ surrendering the right eye of its fighting ability should be painfully abhorrent to us. To lay down our weapons in a covenant with the father of lies is to fall into defeat, slavery, and gross darkness, and it brings reproach upon the church of Jesus Christ!

Agonizing for the Anointing

When the people of Jabesh-Gilead heard the conditions of the covenant, *"all the people lifted up their voices and wept"* (1 Samuel 11:4). Desperation drove them to their knees. Finding oneself in dire need intensifies the spirit in which one prays.

The New Testament, in describing Elijah's prayer to end three years of drought, affirms that *"the effective, **fervent** prayer of a righteous man avails much"* (James 5:16, emphasis added). *Fervent* comes from a word meaning "hot," which accurately described Elijah's supplication. According to *Vine's Expository Dictionary,* that Greek word is similar to the word from which we derive *agonize.* Desperation produces hot, agonizing prayer that accomplishes much.

In regard to my own preaching, I have found by painful experience that my most tried and true sermon is abominably pathetic without the anointing of God. The anointing is to the preacher what ink is to the pen.

God has occasionally left me without the ink of the anointing, and I have had to scrape and scratch to leave any impression upon my hearers. Past experiences have made me desperate for the anointing. If I don't agonize in prayer, I agonize in preaching—and the congregation isn't too far behind.

What, then, is meant by "anointed preaching"? I believe it means preaching that God sees fit to bless—preaching that produces true penitence in the heart of the sinner.

I once read that famous sermon "Sinners in the Hands of an Angry God." When Jonathan Edwards delivered it, sinners were hanging on to the pillars and pews of the building, lest they be swallowed up by hell!

After reading that sermon, I was a little disappointed that I wasn't trembling or laid out on the floor. Why didn't that excellent sermon produce the same results as when it was first preached? Because the anointing of God, not the words of Jonathan Edwards, caused that fearful reaction in the hearts of sinners.

Easy Altar Calls

Without wanting to sound unkind, I think we are "scraping the bottom of the barrel" with modern evangelistic methods. After picking up a book called *Sixty-five Ways to Give an Evangelistic Invitation*, I was dumbfounded by the following suggestions:

> Number 49. Present gifts to those who come forward.

> Number 61. Show a film—keep it dark at the invitation as "some people will come forward more readily in semi-darkness."

After an invitation was given in one church, a Christian gentleman was the first to arrive at the altar. He stood there and winked at the preacher. This man, who had been saved for years, was acting as a drawing card for sinners.

One pastor told sinners that if raising a hand was too difficult during the altar call, just look up and wink. Similar methods that make it easy on the sinner prevent godly repentance from occurring. One pastor excused his methods by saying,

> Things are different nowadays from the days of Finney. People no longer respond in tears, but in joy and gladness.

While I don't judge their converts, I do express grave concern at the lack of contrition at the altar. Both joy and gladness at conversion are two signs of false conversion. (See Matthew 13:20; Mark 4:16.)

How to Get "Decisions"

Years ago I watched an overseas evangelist manipulate a crowd to get decisions for Christ. During that three- or four-day campaign, 217 people decided to follow Jesus. How well were these new believers doing after a period of time? A church member reported that 17 are still going on for Christ. This evangelist, who did not use the Law, created 200 backsliders—quite an achievement for the enemy.

Leonard Ravenhill appropriately said, "Some evangelists are prepared to be anything to anybody as long as they get somebody at the altar for something."

More than once when I have arrived in a city to preach, the pastor has said, "We're believing for plenty of decisions this weekend." My standard reply is, "How many would you like? Ten, twenty, thirty? If you want decisions, I can get them. But if you want to see people saved, that's different—salvation is of the Lord."

On the other hand, if we are quite happy to build our church with decisions, the following are ten tried and true points:

1. Neglect making mention of future punishment.
2. Preach the love of God and the promise of peace, joy, love, and fulfillment.
3. Appeal to the emotions rather than the will and the conscience (address their "loneliness," etc.).
4. Gloss over the seriousness of sin, with "all have sinned."
5. Neglect using the Law of God to bring conviction.
6. For your invitation, use, "While every eye is closed (except one of yours)—nobody is watching you;

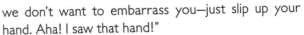

we don't want to embarrass you—just slip up your hand. Aha! I saw that hand!"

7. Have counselors gently pull hand-raisers to the altar (I know a church where it's done).

8. Sing Psalm 119 through three times while you make a final appeal.

9. Use light dimmers.

10. Build your church with the floor sloping toward the front.

You won't have to spend much time agonizing in prayer, because this method works—it doesn't need the anointing! What's more, the time you save in prayer can be devoted to all the counseling you'll have to do. Your church will be transformed into a hive of activity because of all those involved in "follow-up" ministry.

This is called "stony-ground hearer" evangelism, which produces spurious (false) conversions. Many of these "converts" become bitter backsliders, but those who do remain need a "souped-up" church with plenty of activities, or they will slip back into the world.

The Work of the Anointing

In contrast, if we are seeking to build *the* church, we desperately need the anointing of God. In recent years I have laid aside every man-made method of persuasion that has adulterated scriptural evangelism. By God's grace I've preached sin, righteousness, and judgment to the best of my knowledge, pleading with God to anoint His Word. I have not seen multitudes of converts yet, but the results I have seen make me eager for more.

I have seen groups of young people on their knees, with tears streaming down their faces—pretty girls weeping, losing all dignity, not caring what they looked like in the sight of man, but only what they looked like in the sight of a holy God! That is the work of the anointing—I cannot produce contrition.

Holy Spirit conversions put a "must go through Samaria" spirit in the new convert. Such conversions will put a compassion for sinners in the heart of the Christian and make Nahash's covenant seem odious to him. The new believer will then go out to become a soulwinner—a fruit bearer instead of a backslider. Without the anointing, there are few lasting results.

7

Fired Up!

In the previous chapter, we looked briefly at the burden Jesus had for the lost. Look around the body of Christ, and you will see comparatively few with a "must go through Samaria" spirit.

If you contend this fact, here's a way to find out how many really do care for the eternal welfare of sinners. Call a prayer meeting to specifically seek God for the lost. If 15 percent of your church shows up, you're doing well by today's standards.

Oswald J. Smith said, "Oh, my friends, we are loaded down with countless church activities, while the real work of the church, that of evangelizing the world and winning the lost, is almost entirely neglected!"

In this chapter, I think it would be beneficial to ask why our preaching and witnessing lack that desperate zeal.

A great preacher of the past century had these words of regret on his deathbed:

> I have taken a long look into eternity. Oh, if I could come back and preach again, how different I would preach from what I preached before!

Read that again. Let your mind be saturated by the spirit in which he spoke. Each of us needs to look into eternity and then ask ourselves what we are offering this generation—"Things go better with Christ" or salvation from the wrath of a holy God!

A close friend told me of a terrifying dream. God came to him at six in the morning and told him that he had twelve hours to live. He spent those precious twelve hours desperately warning sinners of their need to make peace with God.

When six o'clock came, God said that He had changed His mind, and he could stay. My friend awoke with the cry, "I don't have to go! I don't have to go!" That dream put a desperation in his spirit. Eternity had loomed before him and put a sobriety into his evangelism. I pray God that He would give all of us such dreams—or nightmares!

Fearless Preaching

Paris Reidhead had this to say about John Wesley's preaching:

> Wesley was a preacher of righteousness. He would exalt the holiness of God, the Law of God, the justice of God, the wisdom of His requirements, and the justice of His wrath. Then he would turn to the sinners and tell them of the enormity of their crimes; their open rebellion, their treason, and their anarchy.
>
> The power of God would descend so mightily that it is reliably reported, on one occasion, when the people dispersed, there were eighteen hundred people lying on the ground, completely unconscious because they had had a revelation of the holiness of

God, and in the light of that, they had seen the enormity of their own sin.

Wesley preached the whole counsel of God, and God blessed the word preached with signs following.

Bible commentator A. W. Pink said,

> It is true that there are not a few who are praying for a worldwide revival, but...it would be more timely and more scriptural for prayer to be made to the Lord of the harvest that He would raise up and thrust forth laborers who would fearlessly and faithfully preach those truths which are calculated to bring about a revival. [from *Eternal Punishment*]

God anoints truth.

When George Whitefield preached, tears streamed down his face. While imploring sinners he once said,

> You blame me for weeping; but how can I help it when you will not weep for yourselves, although your own immortal souls are on the verge of destruction, and ought I know, you are hearing your last sermon, and may never have opportunity to have Christ offered to you.

Whitefield gazed into the very fires of hell—*not* into a lost eternity or eternal separation from God. These "fear of man" cliches rob our preaching of its passion. Why let desperation consume us if this is the fate of the ungodly?

The Scriptures speak of the *"lake of fire"* (Revelation 20:14), *"wailing and gnashing of teeth"* (Matthew 13:42), *"where 'their worm does not die, and the fire is not quenched'"* (Mark 9:44). If we really believe in hell, we will plead with sinners.

Years ago a friend called me early in the morning and told me that the building that housed our drug prevention center was on fire. I believed him the moment he spoke. His voice was so earnest!

Catherine Booth said, "If you haven't got tears in your eyes, let them hear tears in your voice!" Her husband knew how to get the tears. His desire was to hang his Salvation Army officers over the fires of hell for a time so they would go out onto the streets with compassion for the lost.

God will keep every promise He has made to the righteous and to the wicked. Those who know the terror of the Lord will persuade men. Spurgeon said, "We need to be ashamed at the bare suspicion of unconcern."

Holy Hatred

In the epic film *Ben Hur,* a new commander comes on board the ship where Judah Ben Hur is a galley slave. As he walks past the broad shoulders of Ben Hur, he swings around without warning and with a whip slashes the bare flesh of Ben Hur's back.

Ben Hur grips the oars, his eyes flashing with emotion. To retaliate would probably mean having his throat cut slowly in front of the crew. Then the commander says, "Your eyes are full of hate, forty-one. That's good. Hate keeps a man alive...it makes him strong. We keep you alive to serve this ship; row well and live."

Look at those words: "Hate keeps a man alive...it makes him strong." The tremendous energy that is contained in hatred can be a powerful motivating force for the kingdom of God. Few Christians, however, realize that we

are commanded to hate. Let's look at several instances in Scripture that justify hate:

> You who love the LORD, hate evil!   (Psalm 97:10)

> Abhor what is evil.   (Romans 12:9)

> The fear of the LORD is to hate evil. (Proverbs 8:13)

Even the perfect Son of God was permitted to hate! Referring to Jesus, the writer to the Hebrews said, "*You have loved righteousness and hated lawlessness*" (Hebrews 1:9). Hatred of sin consumed Jesus and motivated Him to clear the temple.

The Scriptures, however, set boundaries on the way we're permitted to handle our anger and hatred.

> "*Be angry, and do not sin*": do not let the sun go down on your wrath, nor give place to the devil.
> (Ephesians 4:26–27)

> Repay no one evil for evil....Do not avenge yourselves.   (Romans 12:17, 19)

A holy anger needs to be manifested within the church—an anger that finds itself unleashed in passion for souls; an anger that desperately and boldly comes before the throne of grace on behalf of this generation.

In my travels I am beginning to see a glimmer of hope within the church. Different Christians, almost in a whisper of guilt, confide in me that they are getting angry about issues of righteousness such as homosexuality and abortion. I put my hand on their shoulder and say, "That's good, forty-one. Anger shows that you are alive in God."

Getting Our Attention

In the last chapter we looked at Nahash's covenant in which he sought to destroy Jabesh-Gilead's ability to fight. How did King Saul react to the demands of the covenant? *"Then the Spirit of God came upon Saul when he heard this news, and his anger was greatly aroused"* (1 Samuel 11:6). Notice that Saul did not remain passive with his anger:

> So he took a yoke of oxen and cut them in pieces, and sent them throughout all the territory of Israel by the hands of messengers, saying, "Whoever does not go out with Saul and Samuel to battle, so it shall be done to his oxen." And the fear of the LORD fell on the people, and they came out with one consent.
>
> (v. 7)

How did Saul get commitment from the people? He threatened to hew their oxen in pieces. The way to get a man's attention is to touch what is close to his heart. Because oxen were the means of livelihood in those days, the effect was dramatic. The fear of God fell on the people, and they came into a unity of spirit and purpose.

How did God's hewing instrument, Saul of Tarsus, affect the early church? *"Those who were scattered went everywhere preaching the word"* (Acts 8:4). What happened when the hewing process fell on Ananias and Sapphira? *"Great fear came upon all the church and upon all who heard these things"* (Acts 5:11).

A three-month-old convert recently turned up on my doorstep in tears because she was "totally confused." After asking a few questions, this forty-year-old woman admitted she had continued in an adulterous relationship for those three months. I asked her opinion of what God thought of that. "I think He frowns on it, but understands," she sincerely replied. She was lacking in the fear of the Lord—a typical product of the man-centered, "Jesus loves you," "God has a wonderful plan for your life" Gospel.

Squeezing the Church

Some time ago, my cartoonist, Richard Gunther, borrowed my ladder to preach outdoors. As he spoke, he handed out copies of his testimony. A young boy took a copy, stood right in front of my friend, crumpled the testimony, and threw it on the ground.

Something within me snapped! I walked forward, grabbed that kid by the earlobe, and told him that he could crumple my testimony, but not Richard's. Then I squeezed his ear and said, "Now pick up that paper, you litterbug!" I continued to squeeze his ear as we slowly walked to the trash can. *What am I doing?* I thought to myself. *He could have five big brothers!*

The next day that kid was in the front row of the crowd listening to the Gospel! I really don't know if what I did was ethically sound, but one thing I do know: one way to open the ear is to squeeze it!

What does God have to squeeze to get the ear of the church? Does He have to hew our oxen in pieces to give us the fear of the Lord and bring us out in one consent? How long will the church carry on without any real concerned effort to reach the lost? Must we hesitate until judgment begins at the house of the Lord? No, we need not wait. If we chasten ourselves, we will not be chastened.

Don't Hold Back

The very fact that you are reading this book means that you are doing something or are about to do something evangelically. Don't let anything hold you back from sharing your faith. Become familiar with the Scriptures.

> Oh, how great is Your goodness, which You have laid up for those who fear You, which You have prepared for those who trust in You in the presence of the sons of men. (Psalm 31:19)

Realize the liberty we have in Western society. Read Spurgeon's advice on the subject of street preaching and witnessing in the seventeenth century:

> The preachers needed to have faces set like flints, and so indeed they had. John Furz says, "As soon as I began to preach, a man came forward and presented a gun at my face, swearing that he would blow my brains out if I spoke another word. However, I continued speaking and he continued swearing, sometimes putting the muzzle of the gun to my mouth, sometimes against my ear. While we were singing the last hymn, he got behind me, fired the gun, and burned off part of my hair."
>
> After this, my brethren, we ought never to speak of petty interruptions or annoyances. The proximity of a firearm in the hands of a son of belial is not very conducive to collected thought and clear utterance.

Brothers and sisters, how long will we enjoy the freedom we now have? Will you always be able to read a Christian book on evangelism without fear of persecution? Will you always be able to place salvation messages in the local newspaper, pass out tracts on the streets, and speak openly about the salvation of God?

Someone has so rightly said, "The world is dying, the grave is filling, hell is boasting; it will soon be over." We must work while it is yet day!

8

The Way of the Salesman

Some years ago, God led me into drug prevention work. Our means of prevention were twofold:

1. Education regarding licit and illicit drugs.
2. Presenting the Gospel as the answer for prevention as well as rehabilitation.

At one point a non-Christian friend gave me advice that seemed to make sense. He said, "Don't tell people not to take drugs, just mock those who do." This friend of mine was, and still is, extremely anti-Christian, and I found myself in the dilemma of wanting to walk in the counsel of the ungodly.

I could see the truth in what he was saying. In fact, I had used the principle myself many times with those who proudly call themselves atheists. I usually ask, "Did you realize that you are mentioned in the Bible?" Then I show them Psalm 14:1, *"The fool has said in his heart, 'There is no God.'"*

Instead of puffing up the atheist by giving him a title, Scripture mocks the foolishness of his philosophies. Nobody likes to be called a fool. To mock the drug addict and say that only fools abuse drugs was actually a godly principle.

Fools, because of their transgression, and because of their iniquities, were afflicted. (Psalm 107:17)

Fool! This night your soul will be required of you. (Luke 12:20)

In fact, over one hundred examples of such a principle exist in Scripture. Without realizing it, the world often stumbles onto godly principles.

In this chapter we are going to look at "the way of the salesman" in regard to godly principles. These principles may not be the way of every salesman; they are merely my own observations and thoughts on the subject.

Four Principles of Selling

The four principles we are going to discuss are as follows. I call this the R.C.C.R. method:

1. Relate
2. Create
3. Convict
4. Reveal

Principle One: Relate

Let's examine these principles in relation to a vacuum cleaner salesman. His first objective is to make a good first impression with each potential customer. He doesn't want to have the door slammed in his face, so his first words are very important.

Suppose a young mother answers the door. He may say, "Good morning. I'm Mr. Smith from the Cleansweep

Company. I couldn't help noticing your beautiful roses as I walked up your driveway. Are you interested in roses? I'm actually a member of the Rose Garden Society." He may remark about the children or something that gives him a link or a common denominator with the person.

Principle Two: Create

After relating to the woman, the salesman must create an opportunity. To do this, he must deliberately swing to the subject of his product. This is the moment of truth that will reveal whether or not he has a potential customer.

He may say something like, "I have something here I'm sure you, as a homemaker, will be interested in! It's the latest model, straight off the assembly line. You won't believe what it can do!" Enthusiasm grips him. He must give the impression that he believes in the product.

Principle Three: Convict

Next, he must convince her of the superiority of his product, or make her feel bad about her old vacuum cleaner so that she will see the need for a new one. If she is satisfied with her old vacuum cleaner, the salesman must make her unhappy. He may politely ask to see the model she is presently using. When she brings it out, his reaction deserves an Oscar. "Oh, dear! How long have you had that? Ten years— Wow! The motor usually goes after eight years, and when it goes—big bucks!"

Principle Four: Reveal

Now he swings from the negative to the positive, from her old model to his latest one. "Let me just pour this dirt on a portion of your carpet." At this point the salesman may use psychological pressures on the woman by spreading as much material as possible, in as many places as he can. He wants to make her feel a sense of obligation. Why, look at all the trouble this poor man has gone to!

After demonstrating the effectiveness of his new model, he enthusiastically asks, "Have you ever seen anything like that? I'll tell you what I'll do for you; I will give you a generous trade-in on that old model with twelve months to pay."

Quite often salesmen employ a tactic that my daughter used on my wife: "Mom, can I have one or two lollipops?" Notice that Mom wasn't given the choice of yes or no. Before my wife realized that she was not given that option, she responded, "No, you can't have two—one is all you're getting!" And that was all my daughter wanted.

Our salesman doesn't give the young woman the choice of yes or no, but asks something like, "Which sounds better to you, six or twelve months to pay?" or "Which model do you think would be better for this house, the standard or the deluxe?"

The Way of the Master

Before we go any further, let me reiterate my statement at the beginning of this chapter. These principles are godly principles that the world has stumbled onto and perverted. In no way am I insinuating in the following thoughts that Jesus used sales methods to relate to the woman at the well.

As Jesus made His way through Samaria, He anticipated a divine appointment that the Father had planned for Him.

> *So He came to a city of Samaria which is called Sychar, near the plot of ground that Jacob gave to his son Joseph. Now Jacob's well was there. Jesus therefore, being wearied from His journey, sat thus by the well. It was about the sixth hour. A woman of Samaria came to draw water. Jesus said to her, "Give Me a drink."* (John 4:5–7)

Notice that Jesus did not ask, "Are you washed in the blood?" or "Have you crucified your old man?" He related to her on a natural plane because the *"natural man does not receive the things of the Spirit of God, for they are foolishness to him; nor can he know them, because they are spiritually discerned"* (1 Corinthians 2:14).

Dan Wooding, a British journalist now living in Southern California, noted a common pitfall of modern evangelism:

> The big problem is that many Christians speak with forked tongues. They speak a strange lingo called the "language of Zion" and can only be understood by using a special unscrambler, which most reporters do not possess. So we have to learn to speak plainly and not in code.

One of the greatest truths in the Bible is the atoning blood of Christ. Overwhelming the mind of an unbeliever with a spiritual statement early in the conversation, however, is not wise.

Build Bridges, Not Walls

Remember that Jesus did not even mention spiritual matters at first. All He did was ask the woman at the well about something she could relate to—drawing water. Building a bridge with the unsaved is extremely important.

Unbelievers need to see that Christians are genuinely concerned about them. No one wants to feel like he's the target of a religious gunslinger who is out to "save souls."

You may sit next to someone at the beach, park, or local shopping center and just say, "Hi there! Beautiful day, isn't it?" Most people are a little surprised when a stranger speaks to them, but their reaction will betray whether they are cold or warm to you. The more relaxed and friendly you can be, the better. You will have the attention of unbelievers when they discover you can laugh, be friendly, *and* be a Christian!

If they express a measure of warmth, say whatever you feel most comfortable with. Take a genuine interest in people, ask questions, and be a good listener. You may be surprised how many natural conversations turn into witnessing opportunities.

You may not even get onto spiritual topics. If the person has to leave, look on the incident as practice. Make a habit of saying hello to strangers to build up your confidence. Be prayerful, be polite, and be gentle.

Timing and Temperament

Charles Finney gave us some good advice on how to relate to the lost at the proper time:

> Timing is important. You must select a proper time to try to make a serious impression on the mind of a careless sinner. If you fail to select the most proper time, you will most likely be defeated.
>
> It is desirable, if possible, to address a person... when he is away from other activities. It is important to talk with a person when he is not excited about any

other subject. Otherwise, he will not be in the right frame of mind to discuss Christianity.

Be sure that the person is completely sober. Otherwise, he is unfit to be approached on the subject of Christianity. If he has been drinking, you know there is little chance of producing any lasting effect on him.

If possible, when you wish to discuss salvation, talk to a man when he is in a good temper. If you find him in a bad mood, he will probably become angry and abuse you. It is better to leave him alone for that time.

If possible, always take the opportunity to converse with careless sinners when they are alone. Most men are too proud to discuss themselves freely in the presence of others, even their own family.

In visiting families, instead of calling the entire family together at the same time, it is better to see each member one at a time.

Dealing with Discouragement

Never forget that one of Satan's greatest weapons is discouragement. If circumstances don't go right the first time, don't let that concern you. I've had to push many discouraging, frustrating, and embarrassing incidents out of my mind.

I remember showing a couple of non-Christian girls around a church building. Just to relate to them I asked the one who was obviously pregnant, "When are you due?" She said, "I'm not!" Horror gripped me! I just said, "My, what a full dress! Well, I must go. See ya!"

Once I sat next to a hitchhiker in our city square. Just as I decided to ask him where he was from, another unbeliever approached me and began to chat. After a little small talk with him, he went on his way. When I turned to speak to my hitchhiking friend, he was nowhere to be found. I felt a little annoyed. The fish that gets away always seems bigger than the rest.

I eyed another candidate sitting on the other side of the square. As I sat down to join her, I opened our conversation with a remark about the weather. After a few minutes, a gentleman sat between this woman and me and began munching his lunch. Number two had just slipped through my fingers.

Feeling a little indignant, I decided to zero in on the lunch-muncher. This time I determined to at least get a few words in for the kingdom of God. After mentioning the weather, I asked him if he ever listened to the Christians preaching in the square. As he began to answer me, one of the local drunks stood directly in front of us, pointed at Mr. Munch, and bellowed, "Move over!" Shock registered on our faces as we looked up. "Move over!" the drunk repeated in an even louder, brasher tone of voice.

My friend did as he was told. Then this drunk plunked himself down between us and began to sing to me! I couldn't believe what was happening. I just sat there somewhat amused by the situation.

Underneath it all, however, I knew that a battle was raging. Satan doesn't like the steady, resolute fisher of men. He will continually use the seaweed of hindrances and discouragement to thwart our endeavors.

If you have had past failures or discouragement in witnessing, dismiss them from your mind and start afresh. Do

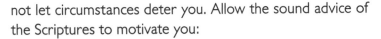
not let circumstances deter you. Allow the sound advice of the Scriptures to motivate you:

> *He who observes the wind will not sow, and he who regards the clouds will not reap....In the morning sow your seed, and in the evening do not withhold your hand; for you do not know which will prosper, either this or that, or whether both alike will be good.* (Ecclesiastes 11:4, 6)

Push Aside Your Fears

A woman once approached me at a seminar and burst into tears. She confessed she had held a long-standing grudge against me because she couldn't witness and I had it "all together." I explained that her assumption just wasn't true, and that I am often terrified when I start witnessing to someone. Even though I have shared my faith many times, Satan continually tries to feed fears into my heart.

Remember that courage is not the absence of fear, but the conquest of fear. If we really care for the ungodly, each of us must learn to push aside fear and replace it with faith in God. You do your part, and God will do His.

The Holy Spirit once prompted me to speak with the next-door neighbor of a pastor in whose home I was visiting. Terror gripped me. "Lord, what am I supposed to say to these people—'God told me to come over and see you'?"

Because the neighbors were into drugs, alcohol, and heavy rock music, I realized they might not exactly welcome a Christian. To find some way to relate to them, I decided to offer them a small gift—a copy of our first publication, *My Friends Are Dying,* a book about drugs.

As I walked up their driveway with the book in hand, a tall man holding a bottle of beer came out onto the patio, pointed at me, and said, "Ray, I just finished reading your book *My Friends Are Dying* three days ago!" He stuck a glass into my hand, put his arm round me, and welcomed me into the house. You do your part, and God will do His.

When We Blow It

Non-Christians seem to wear the helmet of prejudice, with the shield of unbelief, the breastplate of unrighteousness, having their feet shod with how to get away from the Gospel of peace. Nevertheless, we persist, awaiting that willing ear.

At one time or another, everyone has missed an opportunity, suffered a sharp rebuke, or seemingly ruined someone for the Gospel. We need to hand our failures to the Lord and trust Him with the results. Even D. L. Moody was not exempt from the pangs of regret over an encounter with a sinner. The following incident is recorded in *A Treasury of Dwight L. Moody* by Harry Albus:

> One night when Moody was going home, it suddenly occurred to him that he had not spoken to single person that day about accepting Christ. *A day lost,* he thought to himself. But as he walked up the street he saw a man by a lamppost. He promptly walked up to the man and asked, "Are you a Christian?"
> Nor did Moody find soulwinning easy. In fact, even Christians often criticized him for having "zeal without knowledge." Others called him "Crazy Moody." Once when he spoke to a perfect stranger about Christ, the nun said, "That is none of your business...if you were

not a sort of a preacher I would knock you into the gutter for your impertinence."

The next day, a businessman friend sent for Moody. The businessman told Moody that the stranger he had spoken to was a friend of his. "Moody...you've got zeal without knowledge: you insulted a friend of mine on the street last night. You went up to him, a perfect stranger, asked him if he were a Christian."

Moody went out of his friend's office almost brokenhearted. For some time he worried about this. Then late one night a man pounded on the door of his home. It was the stranger he had supposedly insulted. The stranger said, "Mr. Moody, I have not had a good night's sleep since that night you spoke to me under the lamppost, and I have come around at this unearthly hour of the night for you to tell me what I have to do to be saved."

Like Moody, we can trust God with our failures, marvel at His redemption of impossible situations, and rejoice in His faithfulness to bring mankind to Himself.

Failure or Fear of Failure?

Fear of failure, not failure, cripples people. I will never forget my own reaction to the film *Chariots of Fire.* To see a runner fall down, pick himself up, and actually win the race is a tonic for the soul. Nobody wants to be a failure.

We often look at those in our society who hold the gold medal of success in different fields, not realizing that they, too, fell at many a hurdle, yet picked themselves up and kept running.

The mind, not necessarily the body, is the winner. A race car, no matter how powerful, will not win if the driver gives up. The mind is our driving force. Attitude determines success.

You and I should see ourselves as sowers of the good seed, looking for good soil in which to plant. Nothing is wrong with the seed. We will have success if we do our part and plant the seed. Scripture promises that *"those who sow in tears shall reap in joy"* (Psalm 126:5).

Never let failure take your confidence from you. My own father has the attitude that he never fails at squash, he only comes in second. Even in a football game it's important not to lose your confidence after the other team scores. The key is to use that situation to drive you to strive even harder.

The same key of turning the tables on failure is clearly illustrated in the life of David. After David committed adultery with Bathsheba, she conceived and gave birth to a son. Nathan exposed David's sin and prophesied that the child would die.

David fasted and prayed in desperation for seven days. When the child did die, his servants were afraid to approach him with the news. David inquired as to what had happened. When he found out that the child was dead, he got up off the floor, washed, changed his clothes, worshipped God, then had something to eat.

His servants were amazed at his attitude and asked why he had acted that way. His answer speaks volumes.

> *While the child was alive, I fasted and wept; for I said, "Who can tell whether the LORD will be gracious to me, that the child may live?" But now he is dead; why should I fast? Can I bring him back again? I shall go to him, but he shall not return to me.*
> (2 Samuel 12:22–23)

Whether we have been plagued with failures in witnessing or experiences from our past that have left us with an "inferiority complex," they cannot be changed. We need to rise up and follow David's example. Why should yesterday's failures rob us of today's success?

9

When and Where to Witness

When our TV went on the blink, I prayed that God would prepare the serviceman's heart to receive the gospel message. From the moment he introduced himself, I thought his name rang a bell.

He knew that I had preached for many years in the local square outside a large cathedral. As we talked, it dawned on me who he was. This was a man whose neck I could have wrung many times—he was one of the church bell-ringers who had often drowned me out while I was preaching the Gospel!

If you ask God for a woman at the well or a man at the bell, He is faithful. This man was very open, however, and allowed me to take him through the Law. "If you were to touch a wrong wire in the TV and find yourself dead, standing before a holy God, would you be innocent or guilty?" I asked.

He said without hesitation, "Guilty." I asked if his destination would be heaven or hell? He hesitated for what seemed an eternity and then finally stuttered, "Hell." He stood, self-condemned, without excuse. As a result, he was wondrously saved.

The Moment of Truth

Remember the "Way of the Salesman"? Let's look at the second principle given to us in Jesus' discourse with the woman of Samaria. The second principle, *create*, means creating an opportunity. Scripture records the way that Jesus prompted the curiosity of this woman at the well.

> *Then the woman of Samaria said to Him, "How is it that You, being a Jew, ask a drink from me, a Samaritan woman?" For Jews have no dealings with Samaritans. Jesus answered and said to her, "If you knew the gift of God, and who it is who says to you, 'Give Me a drink,' you would have asked Him, and He would have given you living water."* (John 4:9–10)

This was the first time Jesus mentioned spiritual things. Having already related to the woman at the well, He deliberately turned the conversation from the natural to the spiritual. This step is your "moment of truth" that will disclose whether or not your hearer has an ear for the Gospel.

How did the woman at the well respond to Jesus' intriguing mention of "living water"? Her thirst for spiritual truth became obvious.

> *The woman said to Him, "Sir, You have nothing to draw with, and the well is deep. Where then do You get that living water? Are You greater than our father Jacob, who gave us the well, and drank from it himself, as well as his sons and his livestock?" Jesus answered and said to her, "Whoever drinks of this water will thirst again, but whoever drinks of the water that I shall give him will never thirst. But the*

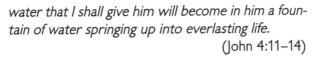

water that I shall give him will become in him a fountain of water springing up into everlasting life.
(John 4:11–14)

Because Jesus aroused her curiosity, the woman at the well expressed interest in the living water that He claimed to have. Without any prompting from Christ, the woman of Samaria said to him, *"Sir, give me this water, that I may not thirst, nor come here to draw"* (v. 15).

This woman was open and ready to hear what Jesus had to say. How can you use Jesus' approach to create an opening in the conversation?

Let's suppose that you've been discussing with a friend the problem of increased violence within our society. You decide to swing to the spiritual by saying, "What this nation needs is a return to Christian principles."

You are seeking to create an opportunity to witness to the person. If this person only could understand that you are not talking about some dead religion, but the gift of God—everlasting life. If the person only knew who Jesus really is, the actual source of life, he would ask you, and you could point him to living water.

This situation can also be compared to a man who has suffered from terrible stomach pains all his life. He has never found any source of relief from his constant agony. Unknown to our ailing friend, the man sitting next to him at a football game is a stomach specialist who has a complete cure to his disorder. If he only knew who he was and what he could give him! If he only knew, he would ask of him.

All humanity agonizes over the fear of death. Jesus Christ is the specialist who alone has the remedy. If only they knew who He was—not just a "great teacher" or a "good man," but life itself.

Contrary to what many people believe, man's strongest desire is not his sex drive, but his will to live, and yet so many are swallowed, screaming in terror, by death's merciless jaws. If they only knew! But they cannot know unless God reveals it to them. God must initiate the process that leads a man to salvation. (See John 6:44.)

If the person you are witnessing to has an open ear, you can be sure that the Holy Spirit is giving him light. Sinners cannot grasp spiritual truth without God's help. Speaking of unbelievers, Scripture says that their understanding is *"darkened, being alienated from the life of God through the ignorance that is in them, because of the blindness of their heart"* (Ephesians 4:18 KJV).

Scripture also reveals the work of God in salvation:

> A certain woman named Lydia heard us. She was a seller of purple from the city of Thyatira, who worshiped God. The Lord **opened her heart** to heed the things spoken by Paul.
> (Acts 16:14, emphasis added)

God gives repentance to the acknowledging of the truth. If the person to whom you are speaking will not give you an ear, just be gentle, prayerful, patient, and polite so that the door is left open for another time. Because salvation is of the Lord from beginning to end, the burden of responsibility does not rest on your shoulders.

You need not feel like a failure if you get a rebuff instead of an opening. This "closed ear" doesn't necessarily mean that God has passed that person by. The Scriptures say that

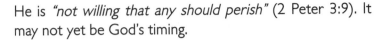

He is *"not willing that any should perish"* (2 Peter 3:9). It may not yet be God's timing.

How to Begin

You may strike up a conversation with someone about the weather, sports, or current events. Then ask the person where he lives or what he does for a living. Be careful, however, that you don't get so deep in conversation that you can't change course. The longer you stay on a topic, the harder it will become to shift gears into the spiritual realm.

I find that the next best thing to do is ask the question, "Do you have a Christian background?" Most sinners answer, "I went to Sunday school when I was a child, but I stopped attending when I got older." Unless you get a sharp rebuke such as "I don't discuss religion or politics, thank you!" you can assume your listener has an open ear.

Then the scriptural question to ask is, "Do you know the Lord?" For many years I asked people if they had ever thought of becoming a Christian. Such a question is offensive to many. To most people a Christian is someone who believes in God and does good to his neighbor. In a sense I was insinuating that the person was atheistic and hated his neighbor.

In our attempt to create an opportunity, we should heed the wisdom related by Charles Finney in his book *Experiencing Revival.**

> When you approach a careless individual, be sure to treat him kindly. Let him see that you are talking with him, not because you seek a quarrel with him,

---

* This book, published by Whitaker House, was formerly published under the name *How to Experience Revival*.

but because you love his soul and desire his best good in time and eternity. If you are harsh and overbearing, you will probably offend him and drive him farther away from the way of life.

Finney went on to say:

> Be serious! Avoid all lightness of manner or language. Levity will produce anything but a right impression. You ought to feel that you are engaged in very serious work that is going to affect the character of your friend or neighbor and probably determine his destiny for eternity. Who could trifle and use levity in such circumstances if his heart were sincere?
>
> Be respectful. Some think it is necessary to be abrupt, rude, and coarse in their discussions with the careless and impenitent. No mistake can be greater. The apostle Peter gave us a better rule on the subject, when he said: *"Be pitiful, be courteous: not rendering evil for evil, or railing for railing: but contrariwise blessing"* (1 Peter 3:8–9 KJV).

When to Witness

I was sitting next to a woman on a plane when the Holy Spirit nudged me to witness to her. An argument began within my mind. I had just preached to a large crowd the night before; surely God didn't expect me to speak to this one woman. Then I smiled with relief because she had just drifted off to sleep.

Within five seconds, the armrest of the seat in front of me fell onto my foot, the food tray fell down and hit my knee, and I choked on a piece of ice that was in my drink! I immediately said to myself, *"Despise not the chastening of the LORD"* (Proverbs 3:11 KJV). I then dropped *Pilgrim's Progress* (which

I was reading) on her foot to wake her, and said, "Oh, sorry about that! Have you read this book?" I discovered that she had, and I was able to witness to her. She was fortunate that I hadn't been reading my Thompson chain-reference foot-breaker!

Many Christians will not witness unless they sense the Spirit of God prompting them to speak to a particular person. I'm not that spiritual. I share my faith whenever and wherever possible. As far as I'm concerned, the starting gun went off more than two thousand years ago with a loud *"Go into all the world and preach the gospel to every creature"* (Mark 16:15).

My conscience continually prompts me to speak. *The Living Bible* renders the new covenant like this: *"I will write my laws in their minds so that they will know what I want them to do without my even telling them"* (Hebrews 8:10 TLB). Danny Lehmann, a personal friend and the author of *Bringin' Em Back Alive,* says, "I think a good rule of thumb to follow would be to presume the Lord wants you to share the Gospel with everyone unless He leads you not to." This is precisely what happened to the early disciples.

> *Now when they had gone through Phrygia and the region of Galatia, they were forbidden by the Holy Spirit to preach the word in Asia. After they had come to Mysia, they tried to go into Bithynia, but the Spirit did not permit them.* (Acts 16:6–7)

They were merely carrying out their commission of taking the Gospel to "every creature," and God in His faithfulness directed their paths.

A friend of mine was once invited to go overseas as a "working missionary" for a short time. He would not only work on the construction of a church building, but he would also be involved in evangelism. He prayed for direction, but it seemed that God wasn't listening. Then he heard of someone else who had been praying for similar guidance. This person prayed and prayed and prayed, and died. My friend took a lesson from the incident, went on that trip, and came back testifying of the providence of God.

When it comes to marriage and other important decisions, we must seek special direction from God. Too often, however, prayer is used to camouflage our lack of activity on behalf of unbelievers. When it comes to reaching out for the lost, go—and pray God's blessing on your labors.

Out of the Salt Shaker

The problem with most Christians is that we tend to mix with the same people each day, not coming into contact with the world as we should. We have taken the command to *"come out from among them and be separate"* (2 Corinthians 6:17) to an extreme. Did you know that the Scriptures actually encourage believers to keep company with sinners? Let's read the apostle Paul's admonition to the Corinthians:

> I wrote to you in my epistle not to keep company with sexually immoral people. Yet I certainly did not mean with the sexually immoral people of this world, or with the covetous, or extortioners, or idolaters, since then you would need to go out of the world. (1 Corinthians 5:9–10)

Christians, like their Master, are to be the friends of sinners. Form an "E" Team—Christians whose hearts are after evangelism. Find a map, pinpoint popular places where

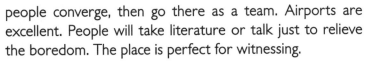
people converge, then go there as a team. Airports are excellent. People will take literature or talk just to relieve the boredom. The place is perfect for witnessing.

You may have botanical gardens, parks, or shopping malls in your city where sinners sit, waiting to be saved. If you need to travel to an ideal location, hire a bus for your team and make a day of it. Make sure they know how to witness using the Law. Take plenty of food, faith, prayer, and good literature. Be a subtle fire-starter.

Salt is useless while it is sitting in an upright shaker. Is your church, youth group, men's or women's group upright but not witnessing? With gentle, prayerful wisdom, and with the help of God, turn them upside down and shake them until they are scattered everywhere preaching the Word.

The opportunities are there. Ask God for creative ways to present the Gospel to the lost and seek His direction. You'll be amazed at how many are hungry and waiting for the message of hope you hold in your heart.

10

Let's Buy the World Lunch

Everyone in town considered me a "fanatic." I had painted the first sixteen verses of John 3 across the front window of my shop. There wasn't even room left for the name of my business!

In 1977 I published an anti-drug pamphlet that received substantial publicity. About a week after publication, my next-door neighbor called me into his barber shop. Before the release of the anti-drug pamphlet, customers would sit down in his chair and say something like, "What a fanatic next door!" Then they would change the subject. But after hearing about the publication, they would say something like, "Doing a good job, that young fellow next door."

What was happening? It was simply an outworking of a scriptural truth: *"For this is the will of God, that by doing good you may put to silence the ignorance of foolish men"* (1 Peter 2:15).

Vegetable Evangelism

After hearing the customers' reaction from the barber, I began to see that good works were a legitimate form of evangelism. With this thought I approached a local gardener and purchased one hundred bags of vegetables. After hearing that I represented a church who wanted to help needy members of the local community, he was very generous. The two-dollar bag of corn, pumpkin, carrots, cabbage, and other vegetables looked rather impressive.

Next, I wrote the following letter, making sure it was free of the usual Christian jargon:

> Dear Neighbor,
>
> We, as a local church, would like to give you the enclosed bag of vegetables as a token of our concern for you. There are no strings attached. There will be no follow-up visit.
>
> If we can help you in any practical way by mowing your lawns, trimming your hedges, etc., please don't hesitate to call on us.
>
> Sincerely,
>
> Pastor Ray Comfort
> New Brighton Christian Center

The vegetables and the letter were dropped at one hundred homes within the immediate area of our local church. Those making the deliveries were instructed not to knock on doors or even get into conversations with the residents. The following are just some of the letters we received from that vegetable drop:

> What a lovely surprise it was to receive those fresh vegetables delivered to my gate. In my thirty years of living in this area, this is the first time anything like this has ever happened. I hope you will be with us for a very long time. It's good to know someone cares.
>
> I wish to thank you very much. I have lived here eleven years—the last nine years on my own—and

have none of my grandchildren or nieces living nearby. I have only one relative left here, and she is over eighty—younger than I am but not as clear in the head.

Although I am an atheist, I appreciate your sincerity and wish you all the best in your efforts in the community.

May I say thank you for the loveliest, most unexpected, and most useful gift I haw ever received. I hope I am a Christian.

I think your organization provides a valuable service, and I admire the results you have achieved. Keep up the good work!

In this day and age it was great to have a Christian organization actually give me something instead of asking me to give to them. I am a very elderly widow, living alone. Your gift was indeed a kind Christian gesture and the first practical act of charity I can remember happening to me.

Many recipients called to thank us. An elderly woman burst into tears of gratitude over the telephone. I was stopped in the street by the neighbors and thanked. One resident, who had lived in the area sixty years, said this was the first time the local church had done anything for her.

A woman, who was saved a short time later, told of her boyfriend walking around the house with a clenched fist, infuriated by the gift, and having no one to argue with.

We found vegetable evangelism to be very fruitful!

The pastor of a church in a small town recently implemented vegetable evangelism. He photocopied the letter

Hell's Best Kept Secret

that was to go with the vegetables at a local store. The shopkeeper read the letter, took a photocopy for himself, and sent it to his son who lived in another town. He included a letter saying, "This is what I call real Christianity." The shopkeeper attended the local church, made a commitment to Christ, and he and his wife (who was also saved) are now missionaries in Nepal.

The Place of Good Works

While some organizations stand accused of going too far into good works, evangelicals as a whole stand guilty, not only of not going far enough, but even of despising this legitimate and scriptural form of evangelism. While it's *"not by works of righteousness which we have done"* (Titus 3:5), Scripture also says, *"I will show you my faith by my works"* (James 2:18).

Rowland Hill said, "I would not give a halfpenny for a man's piety, if his dog and cat were not better off after his conversion." The fruit of good works reveals the true heart of a new convert, giving us grounds for rejoicing in his salvation.

I know that there are batteries in my flashlight when the light shines. Jesus said, *"Let your light so shine before men, that they may see your good works and glorify your Father in heaven"* (Matthew 5:16).

The apostle Paul wrote of those who *"profess to know God, but in works they deny Him, being abominable, disobedient, and disqualified for every good work"* (Titus 1:16). In fact, as one reads the book of Titus, it is a mystery as to how we have missed the message:

> In all things showing yourself to be a pattern of good works. (Titus 2:7)

Jesus Christ, who gave Himself for us, that He might redeem us from every lawless deed and purify for Himself His own special people, zealous for good works.   (Titus 2:13–14)

Remind them to be subject to rulers and authorities, to obey, to be ready for every good work.
                                        (Titus 3:1)

This is a faithful saying, and these things I want you to affirm constantly, that those who have believed in God should be careful to maintain good works. These things are good and profitable to men.
                                        (Titus 3:8)

New Shoes for an Old Soul

During my twelve years of open-air preaching, I have had regular hecklers and quite a bit of opposition. Often things get a little rough. One or two people have spit at or on me, depending on the wind direction. A rather large woman attempted to plunge a syringe into my arm while I was preaching.

One gentleman insisted on shouting out untrue, sexually derogative remarks about my wife. He looked at me after one of these sessions and said, "I bet you hate me." "Are you hungry?" I asked. He looked puzzled. "Have you had lunch yet?" I questioned him. He hadn't, so I took him to a local food store to buy him lunch.

As we stood at the counter I asked him what he wanted. "Just an apple will be fine, thanks," he said meekly. I gave him two. "Like bananas?" "Yes. One will be fine, thanks." I gave him two. Same with oranges. He stood there and said politely, "Thank you very much." Praise God; I had won his heart, not through eloquent words, but through love and for a mere two dollars!

Sometime later I saw this man sitting in the crowd, and I noticed he had bare feet. I asked if he had any shoes. He hadn't, so Sue and I went off to buy him a pair. I had thought a ten-dollar pair from a Salvation Army store would be adequate, but Sue suggested a new pair. We spent forty-three dollars, plus three dollars for a pair of socks.

I then went back to my preaching spot with new shoes in hand, found him, and said, "Here are your new shoes." Normally I am offended by any sort of profanity, but I was amazed at my reaction to his response. He took the shoes and said, !!!**–! He looked at me, then back at the shoes in unbelief and said, !!!**–!

His language didn't worry me. He was totally overcome and was expressing himself the only way he knew how. I kept smiling from ear to ear. I said, "Try them on." As he did, more words to make you hair curl came from his mouth. Once I saw that the shoes fit, I ran off before he could thank me. My countenance was glowing like the noonday sun.

Demonstrating God's Love

Recently I was waiting at an airport when four punks (pathetic unwanted nobody kids) sat next to me. They were typically punk—earrings, tight clothes, bizarre hair styles, and the liberal sprinkling of the four-letter sex verb in their conversation.

I struck up a conversation with them for a few moments, then gave each of them one of our "No Greater Love" evangelical tracts. I actually thought that they would rip them up and curse me, but they took them and began reading. When they said that abortion, adultery, and theft were all right, I told them that their conscience knew right from wrong. That caused one of them to justify himself with, "If I was hungry, I would steal food to live." I said that if he was hungry, he should call me and I would feed him so that he wouldn't have to steal.

It turned out that they were hungry, so I bought them lunch. They couldn't believe it. When one of them asked why I had done it, I said that it was because I liked them.

Suddenly, their manners appeared. They became polite and thankful, saying that it was so good of me. In fact, they thanked me so much it became embarrassing. They ended up taking eleven of our comic tracts, assuring me that they would read them.

Oh, that we would sell our church buildings and buy the world lunch! Why do we spiritualize the feeding of the five thousand? The way to a man's ear is through his mouth.

Do All You Can

It is far more blessed to give than to receive. Giving is almost selfish because of the good feelings it produces. Love your enemies; do good to those who spitefully use you. Need any shoes?

Few of us could claim to have half the zeal for the lost that motivated John Wesley, but listen to his words:

> Do all the good you can, by all the means you can,
> in all the ways you can, in all the places you can, at all
> the times you can, to all the people you can, as long as
> ever you can.

To be rich in good works will not deter the church from fishing for men; it will just give us a well-baited hook: *"Let us not become weary in doing good, for at the proper time we will reap a harvest if we do not give up"* (Galatians 6:9 NIV).

11

Why the Law Works

In the previous chapters, we have looked at two principles used by Jesus in His discourse with the woman of Samaria. First, we need to *relate* to the sinner. The weather, a football game, rising prices, or any subject may be instrumental in building a bridge to him and letting him know that you are a "real" person.

Second, we must *create* an opportunity to gain his attention. This means a deliberate swing to spiritual things. You may make casual mention of a guest speaker at your church, or you may find it easier to hand him a tract or Christian book. This is the "moment of truth"; if he is willing to listen, you can be sure that God is opening his heart.

This brings us to our third point. We must *convict* the sinner. To learn how to do this, let's return to our passage concerning the woman at the well.

> The woman said to Him, "Sir, give me this water, that I may not thirst, nor come here to draw." Jesus said to her, "Go, call your husband, and come here." The woman answered and said, "I have no husband." Jesus said to her, "You have well said, 'I have no husband,' for you have had five husbands, and the one

*whom you now have is not your husband; in that
you spoke truly." The woman said to Him, "Sir, I per-
ceive that You are a prophet."*   (John 4:15–19)

Jesus used the Law of God, specifically the seventh commandment, "You shall not commit adultery," to show her
need of forgiveness.

Let's see how we can use the Law in witnessing to sinners.

Raising the Standard of Measurement

Sinners don't flee from the wrath to come because they
don't believe there *is* a wrath to come. No man in his right
mind would walk into the fires of hell! The whole thought of
God's wrath, Judgment Day, and hell are totally unreason-
able to him.

The reason for this is clearly stated in Scripture.

*For they being ignorant of God's righteousness, and
seeking to establish their own righteousness, have
not submitted to the righteousness of God.*
(Romans 10:3)

The sinner is ignorant of God's righteousness. He has the
audacity to think that God has the same standard as himself.
The wicked receive this rebuke from the Almighty: *"You
thought that I was altogether like you; but I will rebuke you"*
(Psalm 50:21). The sinner has nothing by which to measure
himself. His own standards constantly change. What he tol-
erates morally today, he accepts tomorrow.

The Law changes that by giving him a standard by which
the guilt of his sin can be measured. The Law enlightens
the eyes, enabling the sinner to see the reasonableness of

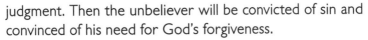

judgment. Then the unbeliever will be convicted of sin and convinced of his need for God's forgiveness.

The Law produces amazing results. You'll find that sinners who are contentious when it comes to eternal issues will actually nod their heads in agreement as you go through each commandment. Their conscience overrides their argument. How does the conscience work in the heart of a sinner?

Contacting Our Ally

During World War II, Britain had powerful weapons, but most of us would agree that it was her allies that actually gave her the victory. The church also has powerful weapons, but God has also given us unseen allies to insure our victory. One of these allies is the Holy Spirit, who reproves the world of *"sin, and of righteousness, and of judgment"* (John 16:8).

Deep within the heart of the sinner, another ally is loyal to our cause. We must know how to contact him so that he can work for us. Who is this faithful ally? He is the ally of the conscience of the sinner.

You have probably watched war movies where the hero is behind enemy lines seeking his contact. He slides up to someone and gingerly whispers, "The blue grass is green on the left side of the yellow fence." The stranger's eyes light up and he gives the corresponding code.

In personal evangelism, Christians are behind enemy lines, seeking to make contact with the ally of the sinner's conscience. This may seem difficult because he may be heavily disguised. Our code is the Law of God. Our ally has been thoroughly briefed. The work of the Law is engraved upon the sinner's heart. His eyes will light up as soon as the code is given.

Dear soldier of the Lord, learn to feed intelligence to the ally of the conscience, and he will shake the human heart to its very foundation. When the Holy Spirit begins dropping the bombs of conviction from above, it won't be long until you have unconditional surrender.

The Work of the Conscience

Conscience is that impartial judge in the courtroom of the mind. He is continually weighing our transgressions and our omissions. The primed conscience should cry "Thief!" at taking a paper clip from the office and "Hypocrite!" for failure to help a stranded motorist. Any of the commandments has the same effect on the human heart. Conscience will then do the rest and strip the sinner of his false peace.

Aim your words at the unbeliever's *will* (his personal responsibility toward God) and the *conscience* (his built-in knowledge of right and wrong). Look at how Spurgeon probed the sinner's conscience:

> O soul! You are at war with your conscience. You have tried to quiet it, but it will prick you. Oh, there are some of you to whom conscience is a ghost haunting you by day and night. You know the good, though you choose the evil; you prick your fingers with the thorn of conscience when you try to pluck the rose of sin.

Because the church has dropped the Law as the means of conviction, few sinners see their need of a Savior. What has been the tragic result? Not too many people want to be saved, mainly because no one warns them that they need to be saved from anything.

In an effort to see souls come to Jesus, many Christians have resorted to psychological manipulation to get decisions. Those who resort to such tactics may find themselves without the help of the Holy Spirit.

When the arrogant lawyer stood up and tempted Jesus and asked Him what he should do to inherit eternal life, Jesus did not lead him in a sinner's prayer. Conviction must precede conversion. This man's attitude obviously showed that he had no sobriety about his sin. His heart was neither broken nor contrite. Jesus, by using the Law, brought a knowledge of the sinfulness of sin. Through the parable of the Good Samaritan, Jesus showed him what the Law actually required, and it left him speechless.

I remember talking to a university student who professed atheism. Her ear was open and, through the use of the Law, I was able to reason with her about the justice of God. She eventually admitted that she was a "praying atheist." This woman, who had been shaking her head in disagreement at my words, was now nodding her head at the truth of God's Word. The Law had made judgment reasonable, or able to be understood.

Appealing to Reason

Conscience and reason walk hand in hand. I find it effective to reason with a sinner over the fact of some recent, horrible crime. For instance, hijackers held a large number of passengers captive in a plane. When their demands were not met, they threw hand grenades and killed most of the men, women, and children.

I ask the sinner how he would react if it had been his father, mother, or other loved one who had been burned alive. Would he demand justice for those murderers? Most will answer a definite "Yes!"

If we mere sinful creatures see the need for justice, how much more does God? Judgment Day is reasonable. The sinner's conscience will affirm that truth.

Listen to Joseph Alleine, a Puritan of the seventeenth century, appeal to the power of reason in the sinner. (I have italicized certain words to emphasize the point):

> If you are men and not senseless stocks, stop and consider where you are going! If you have the *reason* and understanding of men, do not dare to run into the flames, and fall into hell with your eyes open; but stop and think, and set about the work of repentance.... Will you, who are warned, not hasten your escape from eternal torments? Show yourselves men, and let *reason* prevail with you.
>
> Is it a *reasonable* thing for you to contend against the Lord your Maker, or to harden yourselves against His Word, as though the Strength of Israel would lie? Is it *reasonable* that an understanding creature should lose, yea, live quite against the very end of his being?
>
> Is it *reasonable* that the only being in this world that God has made capable of knowing His will and bringing Him glory, should yet live in ignorance of his Maker, and be unserviceable to His use, yea, should be engaged against Him, and spit his venom in the face of his Creator?
>
> Hear, O heavens, and give ear, O earth, and let the creatures without sense judge if this be *reason* that man whom God has nourished and brought up, should rebel against Him? Judge in your own selves....There is

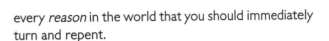
every *reason* in the world that you should immediately turn and repent.

Can you see his continual appeal to the utter foolishness of serving sin and rejecting God's salvation? His appeal is to man's reason because, when the Law is used, judgment is common sense.

The apostle Paul reasoned of sin, righteousness, and judgment when he spoke of salvation to Felix, the governor. Felix trembled because the truth of what Paul said was affirmed by his conscience. The *"work of the law"* was written on his heart, his *"conscience also bearing witness"* (Romans 2:15).

Leading Up to the Law

So now we have before us an open sinner who is willing to listen to our reasonings. We have mentioned Christian things, and he hasn't turned us off. We know a little about his spiritual condition because of the question, "Do you have a Christian background?"

Having allowed you to dig thus far, he should not find your next query offensive. This question is the springboard to the Law: "Do you see your own need of God's forgiveness?" Most will answer, "Not really."

From there I usually lead into the Law using my own testimony by saying something like, "I felt the same way before I became a Christian. I didn't see myself as being a particularly bad sinner because I measured myself by man's standard."

I often tell the story of a little girl who remarked to her mother how clean some sheep looked against the green grass. Then, as snow began to fall, this same girl noticed how dirty the sheep looked against the white snow. The background made all the difference.

If you and I judge ourselves using the background of human standards, we come up quite clean. We can find plenty of people who are worse than us. The average sinner looks almost pure compared to Adolf Hitler, for example. God, however, will not judge us using human standards, but by the absolute standard of His Law, the Ten Commandments.

Until the snow fell, the girl didn't know what real purity was. If we don't let the snow of the Law of God fall upon the sinner, he will have no gauge by which to measure himself. "All have sinned" does not tell him how much he has sinned. Only the Law does that. Let me illustrate.

The Priceless Vase

A young boy was once told by his father that a certain vase was priceless. The child was forbidden to touch it or even go near the glass case in which it was displayed.

During a trip to the store a few months later, the boy noticed an identical vase that cost only five dollars. From then on, not only did the son doubt his father's credibility, but he also lost all reverence for that "priceless" vase.

In fact, while his father was out one day, the boy decided to take a closer look at the vase. He unlocked the glass door and carefully handled the family heirloom. This vase was much lighter than the one in the supermarket, but there was no doubt about it—it was identical!

As he pondered why his father would lie to him about its value, he heard a car pull up the driveway. In his haste

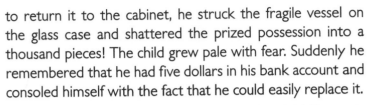

to return it to the cabinet, he struck the fragile vessel on the glass case and shattered the prized possession into a thousand pieces! The child grew pale with fear. Suddenly he remembered that he had five dollars in his bank account and consoled himself with the fact that he could easily replace it.

When the father entered the house, the child flippantly called out, "Dad, I broke that vase thing in the cabinet. It's okay, though. I can get another one at the store with the five dollars I've got in the bank."

His father turned pale with solemnity. Without a word, he approached his son, placed his hands on the boy's shoulders, looked him in the eyes, and said with trembling voice, "Son, that was no cheap imitation vase. That was an antique worth twenty-five thousand dollars!"

Suddenly the seriousness of the boy's disobedience hit him. His mouth went dry. Tears welled in his eyes. He broke down with uncontrollable sobbing, fell into his father's arms, whispering in bitter lamentation, "I'm sorry....I'm sorry!"

His father gently wiped the child's tears and said, "Son, there's no way you are going to be able to pay for that vase. It's going to take everything I've got, but I'll pay for a new one myself."

Conflicting emotions gripped the child—on one hand horror that his father would go to such expense, and on the other hand gratitude that he would do such a thing for him despite his deliberate disobedience. Unutterable relief and unspeakable appreciation consoled his grief.

A Question of Value

Let's now ask a number of relevant questions about the incident. First, what brought sorrow to the child? He felt no remorse for his actions until his father solemnly explained the *value* of the vase and the *cost of replacement*.

The boy could never raise that amount of money. Not only did he lack means of payment, but the seriousness of his crime and the stark reality of his disobedience drove him to cry out in despair. He had no other option but to fling himself upon the mercy of his father.

Second, did the father have to break the child's toys to make him sorry for his disobedience? No, the child's possessions and his attitude toward them were, at that point, irrelevant to the situation. The father brought before the child the *seriousness* of his transgression by speaking of the value of the vase and the cost of its replacement. If he had been overly affectionate toward his toys previously, after such a demonstration of love from his father, no doubt he would have put them into a right perspective.

Third, what would have been the outcome if the child had broken the vase, but the father responded differently? Suppose when the father came home, the boy flippantly called, "I broke the vase thing, but my five dollars will pay for a new one." The father called back, "Son, there's no way you can afford to buy a new one. I'll pay for it myself."

If the father failed to soberly explain the value of the vase and the cost of replacement, his son would lack three crucial attitudes:

1. Genuine sorrow for what he had done
2. Esteem for the replacement vase
3. Appreciation of what his father had done

How to Produce Godly Sorrow

Being alienated from the life of God through the ignorance that is in him, the blind, unregenerate child of disobedience thinks lightly of sin. There is no fear of God before his eyes. Lust, pride, and selfishness are part of his everyday life. His attitude is, "Nobody's perfect!" His five dollars of self-righteousness appeases his accusing conscience.

Yet, as we have seen previously, God has graciously placed within the reach of the church a tool to awaken the sinner to his plight. God has a way to parade before him the value of the vase of the divine Law. For the sinner to produce godly sorrow, we must show him three truths:

1. The value of the Law; that it is holy, just, good, and perfect. (See Romans 7:12; Psalm 19:7.)

2. That he has broken that Law into a thousand pieces, for *sin* is the transgression of the Law. (See 1 John 3:4.)

3. That divine wrath issues from the judgment bar of almighty God toward him; that his five dollars of self-righteousness may appease his guilty conscience, but it cannot appease eternal justice. (See John 3:36.)

Remember, the father didn't need to break his child's toys to produce genuine sorrow. Breaking his son's toys would have produced sorrow but not repentance. When the father demonstrated the seriousness of the transgression by stating the value of the vase and the cost of replacement, conscience did the rest.

In the same way, the sinner's state of happiness, the worth of his possessions, and the size of his bank balance have little or no bearing on whether or not he will repent.

Economic collapse or tragedy may make a man listen, but it may not make him repent. A sinner may respond to disaster with bitterness or sorrow—but not necessarily godly sorrow. As with the child, the sinner's material possessions will be put in perspective after seeing the love of God demonstrated in Calvary.

The "doom and gloom" message of having to see things get worse before God brings revival has been with the church for some time now. Some Christians mistakenly believe that men will not repent while they are happy. But what really causes men to come to Christ?

We must see that the Law, not tragic circumstances, brings men to salvation. Difficulties may get a man's attention, but the Law is still necessary to drive him to Christ.

The Sickle of the Law

Jesus didn't push the great harvest of souls into the future, awaiting economic collapse or any other event. He spoke of the harvest as being present.

> Do you not say, "There are still four months and then comes the harvest"? Behold, I say to you, lift up your eyes and look at the fields, for they are already white for harvest! (John 4:35)

The problem isn't that sinners are too happy to repent, but that the church has failed to pick up the sickle of the Law! When we, like the apostle Paul, preach sin, righteousness, and judgment by the Law, we work with the Holy Spirit, who convicts of sin, righteousness, and judgment. (See John 16:8.)

Instead of playing on the sinner's emotions, we appeal to the *"work of the law"* written in his heart (Romans 2:15), thus annihilating his self-righteousness. Yet there is little or no preaching of divine wrath or of future punishment.

Preaching grace alone, or the work of the cross with no reference to Law, has left the sinner thinking lightly of sin. We have circumnavigated the very evangelical essential, which is the instrument of God to produce contrition.

By preaching solely the good news that the Father paid all in Christ, that *"Christ has redeemed us from the curse of the law"* (Galatians 3:13), we have left the sinner totally ignorant of that very Law! How, then, can he find repentance? The result has been a lack of contrition, a lack of repentance, and a lack of zeal to evangelize. And the horrible tragedy is that without repentance, there is no salvation. (See Matthew 3:7–10; Luke 13:3.)

For too long the god of this world has hidden the sickle from the laborers. Learn how to go through the essence of the Law by preaching what each commandment actually demands in the light of New Testament revelation.

God is seeking those who will reach out in fervent prayer to grip that sharp sickle by the handle of faith. You can experience the joy of watching it reflect the pure light of the Word of God. You can see the Law, with the razor-edge of a surgeon's blade, cut deep into the heart of the harvest, thus bringing true repentance and with it sound conversions, to the honor of God.

12

Ten Steps to Conviction

The way to produce conviction in the heart of a sinner is to take him through the Ten Commandments. (See Exodus 20:1–17.) As we do so, see if you could stay alive after each barrel blasts you; watch how the Law annihilates self-righteousness.

1. You shall have no other gods before Me. That means that we should love God with all our heart, mind, soul, and strength.

Jesus brought out the essence of the command by saying, *"If anyone comes to Me and does not hate his father and mother, wife and children, brothers and sisters, yes, and his own life also, he cannot by My disciple"* (Luke 14:26). This is what is commonly called a hyperbole, that is, contrasting love with hate for emphasis. Our love for our Creator, the One who gave us life, should be so great that all our other affections should seem as hate in comparison to it.

Many years ago, I bought a color television so that my children could watch afternoon children's programs. The first day we had the set, I arrived home and noticed that my offspring weren't at the door to greet me. They were glued to the TV. My homecoming had become a non-event.

I walked over to the television, turned it off, and said, "Kids, I bought that TV for your pleasure, but if it comes between you and your love for me, it's going. It's a wrong order of affections. You are setting your affection on the gift, rather than the giver."

In the same way, if we love husband, wife, child, boy-friend, girlfriend, car, sports, motorbike, music, or even our own lives more than we love God, we are setting our affections on the gift rather than the Giver. It is a wrong order of affection, which the Bible calls "inordinate affection." God is jealous for our love. He should be the focal point of our lives and affection.

In my twenty-two years as a non-Christian, I certainly didn't love God with heart, mind, soul, and strength; in fact, His very name epitomized the word *boredom* to me. When the truth was shown to me, I knew I had miserably failed to keep the first commandment.

2. You shall not make for yourself any carved image. This speaks of those who *"changed the truth of God into a lie"* (Romans 1:25 KJV). Multitudes make God into their own image by saying, "My God is a God of love; He would never create hell."

The irony of it is that they are right. Their god would never create hell, because he doesn't exist! He is a figment of their vain imaginations, shaped to conform to their sins. Their gods don't have commandments or moral dictates because they are dumb. *"Those who make them* [idols] *are like them; so is everyone who trusts in them"* (Psalm 115:8).

If a man walked down a railway track, saw a train racing toward him, closed his eyes, and said, "I believe it's a marshmallow train," would it change reality? No. What he believes doesn't matter. What matters is that if he doesn't get off the track, *he* will be a marshmallow!

The truth is that it doesn't matter what we believe about God. He says, *"I am the LORD, I do not change"* (Malachi 3:6). The Bible warns that idolaters will not inherit the kingdom of God. (See 1 Corinthians 6:9.)

3. You shall not take the name of the Lord your God in vain, for the Lord will not hold him guiltless who takes His name in vain. Jesus said, *"For every idle word men may speak, they will give account of it in the day of judgment"* (Matthew 12:36).

I was once sitting at a restaurant counter near two young ladies who were talking. After about five minutes I leaned across and offered one of the girls a booklet. She noticed that it was a Christian booklet and said that she was a Christian. I turned to her friend and said, "You're not, though, are you?"

She replied, "Why do you say that?"

I gently answered, "Because in the past five minutes, you've blasphemed God's name four times."

She put her hand to her mouth and said, "God...I have!"

To which I said, "Five!"

I explained, "When a man hits his thumb with a hammer, he may express his pain and disgust by using a four-letter word. Then again, he may use the name of God. When he does, he takes the name that is above every name, that holy name of his Creator, and brings it down to the level of a four-letter filth word!"

Then, in gentleness I said to her, "That's called blasphemy, and I wouldn't be in your shoes on Judgment Day for all the tea in China!" She looked me straight in the eye and said, "You've ruined my day!" She was really upset. The work of the Law was written in her heart.

4. Remember the Sabbath day, to keep it holy. In retrospect, I failed to give God even one minute's worship in twenty-two years as a non-Christian, much less one day in seven.

Even though He gave me eyes, ears, a mind, the power of reason, and life itself, I never bothered to say, "O God, You gave me life. What do You require of me?"

5. Honor your father and mother. Who can say that he's kept this command? The word *honor* means "to value." God's idea of value and ours, no doubt, are poles apart. Ephesians 6:2 says this is the first commandment with promise. Therefore, if it is broken, all will *not* be well with you, and your days will *not* be long upon the earth.

God gave some stern warnings in the Old Testament to children who refused to honor their parents.

> *If a man has a stubborn and rebellious son who will not obey the voice of his father or the voice of his mother, and who, when they have chastened him, will not heed them, then his father and his mother shall...say to the elders of his city, "This son of ours is stubborn and rebellious; he will not obey our voice; he is a glutton and a drunkard." Then all the men of his city shall stone him to death with stones; so you shall put away the evil from among you, and all Israel shall hear and fear.* (Deuteronomy 21:18–21)

The eye that mocks his father, and scorns obedience to his mother, the ravens of the valley will pick it out, and the young eagles will eat it. (Proverbs 30:17)

6. You shall not murder. Scripture says, *"Whoever hates his brother is a murderer, and you know that no murderer has eternal life abiding in him"* (1 John 3:15). The New Testament does not deal with only outward actions, but also the inward motivations of our hearts.

Jesus made this piercing statement:

You have heard that it was said to those of old, "You shall not murder, and whoever murders will be in danger of the judgment." But I say to you that whoever is angry with his brother without a cause shall be in danger of the judgment. And whoever says to his brother, "Raca!" shall be in danger of the council. But whoever says, "You fool!" shall be in danger of hell fire. (Matthew 5:21–22)

Hatred, unholy anger, and name-calling put us in danger of hell's fires as surely as if we had taken a gun and murdered the person.

7. You shall not commit adultery. Like the above command, the New Testament reveals the essence of God's pure standards. Jesus said that *"whoever looks at a woman to lust for her has already committed adultery with her in his heart"* (Matthew 5:28).

In civil law, to conspire to commit a crime can be as much a transgression as the committal of the crime itself. God knows that he who lusts holds back from adultery not for conscience' sake but for lack of opportunity. Adulterers will not inherit the kingdom of God. (See 1 Corinthians 6:9.)

8. You shall not steal. No thief shall enter the kingdom of God. What do you have to steal to be a thief? A paper clip will do, or failure to pay taxes. If you have taken anything that doesn't belong to you, no matter how small, you won't enter the kingdom of God! (See 1 Corinthians 6:10.)

Both Old and New Testaments describe not only sins of commission, but also sins of omission. If we have failed to meet a need with our resources, are we not as guilty as if we have stolen from the less fortunate?

> Do not withhold good from those to whom it is due, when it is in the power of your hand to do so. Do not say to your neighbor, "Go, and come back, and tomorrow I will give it," when you have it with you.
> (Proverbs 3:27–28)

> Therefore, to him who knows to do good and does not do it, to him it is sin. (James 4:17)

Stealing from the less fortunate by our inactivity is a crime in God's sight. Many people have never considered that their lack of generosity is also robbing God of what is rightfully His.

> Will a man rob God? Yet you have robbed Me! But you say, "In what way have we robbed You?" In tithes and offerings. You are cursed with a curse, for you have robbed Me, even this whole nation.
> (Malachi 3:8–9)

9. You shall not bear false witness against your neighbor. This is more commonly known as telling "fibs" or "white lies." Lying also includes making exaggerated claims.

Remaining silent to falsely take credit for the accomplishment of another is also wrong. A subtle change in tone, inflection, or expression can be as misleading and untruthful as the boldest lie.

Anyone who lies sides with satan himself—the father of lies. The Bible says—and Scripture *cannot* be broken—*"All liars shall have their part in the lake which burns with fire and brimstone"* (Revelation 21:8).

10. You shall not covet. This means not to be greedy or materialistic. The covetous will not inherit the kingdom of God. (See 1 Corinthians 6:10.) Instead of always grasping for more, we ought to be satisfied with what we have. The apostle Paul encouraged us, *"Godliness with contentment is great gain....And having food and clothing, with these we shall be content"* (1 Timothy 6:6, 8).

"For whoever shall keep the whole law, and yet stumble in one point, he is guilty of all" (James 2:10). Those who still cling to a few fig leaves of self-righteousness will despair of their efforts in light of this truth—the final nail in the coffin. You don't have to break ten civil laws to have the police after you. Just break one and you are a lawbreaker in debt to the law.

Speaking with Anxious Sinners

Can you see how the Law makes the fact of hell reasonable? I have seen sinners utterly deny the existence of hell until I took them through the Law. The Law not only makes sinners tremble, but it makes them miserable. How can a man enjoy the pleasures of sin, knowing that the eye of a holy, wrath-filled God abides upon him?

I once preached a series of seven meetings. On the last, a miserable young man approached me and said, "These past seven days have been the worst days of my life, thanks to you!" I was greatly encouraged.

Miserable and trembling though a sinner may be, this doesn't necessarily mean he is repentant. Governor Felix trembled, but he didn't want to let go of his sin. He didn't cry out, "What, then, must I do?" He was "open" but not "anxious." If the apostle Paul had been able to get a "decision," no doubt it would have been spurious.

How can you tell the difference between an open sinner and an anxious one? Someone under conviction will typically become fidgety and hang his head like a child who has been in his disobedience. Charles Finney, in his book *How to Experience Revival,* gave some excellent advice on how speak with anxious sinners:

> Bring up the individual's *particular sins.* Talking in general terms against sin will produce no results. You must make a man feel that you mean *him.* A minister who cannot make his hearers feel that he means them cannot expect to accomplish much. Some people are very careful to avoid mentioning the particular sins of which they know the individual to be guilty, for fear of hurting his feelings. This is wrong. If you know his history, bring up his particular sins. Kindly but plainly, not being offensive, awaken his conscience and give full force to the truth.
>
> Be sure to *be very plain.* Do not cover up any part of the person's character or his relationship to God. Lay it all open, not to offend or wound him, but because it is necessary. Before you can cure a wound, you must probe it to the bottom. Keep back none of the truth, but let it come out plainly before him.

No Shortcuts

The Christian is very much like the honey bee. Watch a bee at work. He is intent on finding nectar. He goes from flower to flower in search of that precious substance. When he finds some, he goes to the very heart of the flower. Christians must continually search for the nectar of an open heart in unbelievers.

If we discover the nectar of an open heart, we take the sinner through the Law to convict him. Then, if the sinner becomes "anxious" under conviction, by God's grace, we convert him. If his heart is open but the sinner is unconcerned about the state of his soul, we sting him with the Law, then buzz off. We are ministers of the honey of grace or the sting of judgment; the goodness or the severity of God; a savor of life or the savor of death.

Remember that all our efforts are utterly futile without the conviction of the Holy Spirit—*"Unless the LORD builds the house, they labor in vain who build it"* (Psalm 127:1).

Notice, to this point, that I have not mentioned the cross. First the sinner must be brought to a point of crying, "What, then, must I do?" If he doesn't see his guilt before God and that he is totally deserving of His wrath, there will be no genuine contrition, no real repentance, no gratitude for forgiveness, and therefore no zeal to do the will of God.

To shortcut the need to convict the sinner, in both personal witnessing and preaching, will reap nothing but a harvest of stony-ground hearers who will become bitter backsliders—but not before they have created great havoc the church.

13

Time to Talk about Jesus

Because I travel a great deal by plane, experience has shown me that the best seat in a Boeing 737 is seat 3B. Why is it the best seat? There are several reasons. It's at the front of the plane, and you are first to be served with tea or coffee. You also have plenty of leg room since there are no seats in front of you. The magazines are close at hand, and you are first to be offered candy. You are first to leave the ground and first to arrive. Engine noise is low because the engines are behind you.

Best of all, he who sits in 3B has 3A and 3C to witness to. On one recent trip I began to chat to 3A, using the R.C.C.R. method. I asked about the gentleman's job. He worked as a manager with the railroad. After relating to him, I waited to create an opportunity to mention Christian things. He mentioned a particular suburb where I knew a vibrant church was located. So I asked him if he was familiar with it. He wasn't. "Do you have a Christian background?" His reply was clear—"Nope!" By his attitude I could see that he wasn't open.

Next, I turned to 3C. I asked her what she had been doing in the city we had just left. She had been skiing. We discussed the joys of the sport for several minutes. Then she asked me my occupation. This was my chance to create an opportunity to mention Christian things.

I told her that I write Christian books, then asked her if she had a Christian background. She said she had. Did she see herself as a sinner in God's sight? She didn't. I said that for years I didn't until I saw the standard with which God was going to judge the world on Judgment Day. Then one by one, we went through the Ten Commandments.

Suddenly she began to see sin for what it was. She said, "That's what I've been doing. I've been measuring myself by man's standard!" Tears welled up in her eyes as I shared that Christ has redeemed us from the curse of the Law. The Gospel made sense to her. She asked what she should do, and I had the joy of leading her to the Savior as the plane began to land.

I inquired as to whether she had a Bible and if she knew any Christians. She did have a Bible, and a Christian at work had been sowing seed. God usually orchestrates a number of encounters with laborers before a person comes to Christ.

> *For in this the saying is true: "One sows and another reaps." I sent you to reap that for which you have not labored; others have labored, and you have entered into their labors.* (John 4:37–38)

When the Law is used, John 4:35 begins to make sense:

> *Do you not say, "There are still four months and then comes the harvest"? Behold, I say to you, lift up your eyes and look at the fields, for they are already white for harvest!*

The problem hasn't been with the harvest, but with the reapers. Christians have neglected to pick up the sickle of the Law!

Time to Reveal Jesus

So far we have studied the first three steps involved in witnessing and evangelism.

> 1. *Relate*—the need to relate to the sinner on the natural level, before we speak of spiritual things.
>
> 2. *Create*—the necessity of creating an opportunity to witness, by deliberately swinging from the natural to the spiritual. This is our "moment of truth" when we find out if we have the ear of the person.
>
> 3. *Convict*—the importance of using the Law of God to make judgment reasonable to the sinner.

Now let's look at the fourth point. We must *reveal* who Jesus Christ is and His finished work of the cross.

Each of these four points is based on John chapter four. Jesus related to the woman of Samaria, created an opportunity, brought conviction, and then revealed Himself to her with the words, *"I who speak to you am He"* (John 4:26).

What we have been attempting to do, with the help of God, is bring the sinner to a point of crying, "What must I do?" He has suddenly seen that Judgment Day is not only reasonable, but also inevitable. The Law has given him light, which is confirmed by his conscience. As the Holy Spirit illuminates his mind, he begins to tremble. Hell opens wide its jaws. He looks to you for direction. Now what do you do?

After revealing the person and work of Christ to the sinner, you can help him put his faith in Jesus for salvation.

Use the following Scriptures to show him that Jesus Christ is God come in the flesh:

> In the beginning was the Word, and the Word was with God, and the Word was God....And the Word became flesh and dwelt among us. (John 1:1, 14)

> Then He [Christ] said to Thomas, "Reach your finger here, and look at My hands; and reach your hand here, and put it into My side. Do not be unbelieving, but believing." And Thomas answered and said to Him, "My Lord and my God!" (John 20:27–28)

Only by living a perfect and sinless life could Christ be worthy to bear our sin upon the cross. Scripture says that God *"made Him [Christ] who knew no sin to be sin for us, that we might become the righteousness of God in Him"* (2 Corinthians 5:21). Christ suffered the penalty for sin that rightfully belonged to us. As a result of His sacrifice, Christ offers us abundant life right now and the assurance of everlasting life. *"But the gift of God is eternal life in Jesus Christ our Lord"* (Romans 6:23).

Once the sinner acknowledges who Christ is and what He did, how does he take hold of saving faith in God? For the answer to this question, let's examine the Scriptures.

What Must I Do to Be Saved?

On their way to the place of prayer in Philippi, Paul and Silas encountered a girl with a spirit of divination. This demonically possessed person brought her masters much revenue by fortune-telling. The girl followed Paul and Silas shouting, *"These men are the servants of the Most High God, who proclaim to us the way of salvation"* (Acts 16:17).

Satan in his subtlety sought to bring confusion to the Gospel by aligning it with divination. The girl continued to shout this way for many days. The apostle Paul, being grieved, finally commanded the spirit to come out of her, and it did.

The masters of the girl saw that their means of livelihood had also been cast out, so they seized Paul and Silas, had them severely beaten, and threw them into prison, *"commanding the jailer to keep them securely. Having received such a charge, he put them into the inner prison and fastened their feet in the stocks"* (Acts 16:23–24).

At midnight, as Paul and Silas prayed and sang praises to God within the hearing of the other prisoners, a great earthquake occurred. The Bible tells us that *"the foundations of the prison were shaken; and immediately all the doors were opened and everyone's chains were loosed"* (v. 26).

The jailer awoke, saw the open doors, thought that the prisoners had gone, and drew out his sword to kill himself. Then Paul called out that no one had escaped and that he was not to do himself any harm. The jailer came in trembling and fell down before Paul and Silas, asking the crucial question, *"Sirs, what must I do to be saved?"* (v. 30).

Now look at their answer: *"Believe on the Lord Jesus Christ, and you will be saved, you and your household"* (v. 31). Then the disciples spoke the Word of the Lord to him and to all who were in his house. And as they had prophesied, his whole family received the Gospel and were baptized the same hour of the night.

Paul and Silas told that awakened, trembling sinner to believe on the Lord Jesus Christ. What does that mean?

Believe means to trust in, rely on, and cling to the person of Jesus Christ alone for salvation. It does not mean to believe on Him as a historical figure. It does not mean to trust Christ only in the midst of sickness or financial needs. Temporal faith, like mere intellectual assent, is insufficient to gain access to heaven.

The jailer was not told to acknowledge that God's true name is Jehovah, to be baptized into a certain church, or to keep a certain day. He was told to trust in Jesus. Why? Because *"he who has the Son has life"* (1 John 5:12).

This jailer was obviously penitent. He had conviction of sin. Humility was evidenced by his attitude to the disciples, falling at their feet and calling them "sirs." He was conscious of the wrath of God and the urgency of his plight, evidenced by the words *"must"* and *"saved."*

Suppose the Holy Spirit and the use of the Law have brought a sinner, like the Philippian jailer, to conviction. Unfortunately, many Christians hesitate to ask for a commitment at this crucial point. Why do we hedge? First because the sinner may reject the offer of salvation. We must learn to disassociate ourselves from the gospel message, presenting it as the Truth that demands a decision. If the sinner refuses the Truth, we must not take his rejection of our message as a rejection of us personally.

Another reason Christians shy away from asking for a commitment involves fear on our part. We are afraid the sinner may actually accept the offer of salvation. We think, "Now what do I do?" and panic. Most Christians have never personally led anyone to Christ, so a positive response by the sinner often launches the believer into unknown waters.

Many souls are won or lost at this awkward and often unexpected moment in witnessing. That's why it's crucial to be prepared—like Paul and Silas were—to gently lead a sinner in a verbal expression of his new commitment.

The sinner may be too embarrassed to pray on his own initiative, so you may offer to lead him in prayer. Remember to emphasize the basics of salvation as you pray. The following prayer can be a guide:

Dear God,

I acknowledge that You are holy, righteous, and just. I confess my sinfulness to You; I have repeatedly broken Your Law and deserve eternal punishment. Forgive me for my sin, and give me the grace to turn from my selfishness and rebellion.

Thank You for taking my place on the cross as punishment for my sin. I receive You as Lord and Savior. Please give me the grace to live the kind of life that will glorify You in all that I say and do. In Jesus' name. Amen.

Now What?

Suppose you have had the thrill of leading someone to Christ. Now what do you do? First, suppress the urge to tell him that he's saved. If God has saved him, let God tell him. Show him the promises of assurance, of course, but allow his assurance to come from God alone.

The Spirit Himself bears witness with our spirit that we are the children of God. (Romans 8:16)

He who believes in the Son of God has the witness in himself. (1 John 5:10)

A well-known preacher was once walking through the streets of London when a drunk bumped into him. The drunk took one look at the preacher and said, "Do you remember me?" The preacher said that he didn't. The drunk looked at him and said, "Well you should—I'm one of your converts!" The preacher looked sternly at the man and said, "That may well be; but if you were one of God's converts, you wouldn't be in such a state!"

In times of testing, the new believer must rely on the truth of the Scriptures and the inner witness of the Spirit that he has been converted—not the words of a mere man.

Encourage this new saint to memorize and meditate on the Word of God. Two Scriptures that are especially helpful for the new believer are:

> *I will never leave you nor forsake you.*
> (Hebrews 13:5)

> *If we confess our sins, He is faithful and just to forgive us our sins and to cleanse us from all unrighteousness.* (1 John 1:9)

Next, you'll want to instruct him in the basic principles of the Christian faith.

1. Have faith in God. A young man told me that some of the things in the Bible were "hard to believe." I asked him his name. When he told me I quipped, "I don't believe you." He looked puzzled. I asked him again, and when he told me, I said the same thing. His eyes flashed with anger. He reacted that way because my lack of faith in him had insulted him. I had insinuated that he was a liar.

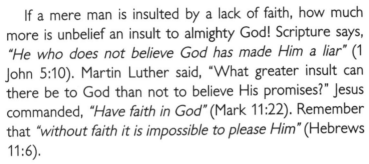

If a mere man is insulted by a lack of faith, how much more is unbelief an insult to almighty God! Scripture says, *"He who does not believe God has made Him a liar"* (1 John 5:10). Martin Luther said, "What greater insult can there be to God than not to believe His promises?" Jesus commanded, *"Have faith in God"* (Mark 11:22). Remember that *"without faith it is impossible to please Him"* (Hebrews 11:6).

2. Read the Word of God daily. Read the Bible without fail, obeying implicitly what you read. Take the time to read Psalm 1, then read Psalm 119 until you get the message about daily meditation on the Word. If you do not discipline yourself to feed on the Word daily, you will join the ranks of those who suffer from spiritual malnutrition. Satan has great success stomping on sickly saints.

3. Fellowship. Find a good, loving, Bible-based church and commit yourself to their vision. Scripture admonishes us not to forsake *"the assembling of ourselves together"* (Hebrews 10:25). Whatever you do, don't let yourself get involved with murmurers in the church.

4. Water baptism. Seek to be water baptized without delay. This is a command of Scripture. Water baptism parallels what has actually happened to you in the spiritual realm—you have died, been buried, and are raised in Christ.

5. Be filled with the Spirit. There is some controversy within the body of Christ about different experiences people say have had with the Holy Spirit. However, there is no denial that *all* Christians are commanded to *"be filled with Spirit"* (Ephesians 5:18). You should be willing fish, deep in the ocean of the Spirit of God. You are told not only to be led with the Spirit, but also to walk in the Spirit, live in the Spirit, sow to the Spirit, mind the things of the Spirit, and be led by the Spirit (Romans 8:5, 14; Galatians 5:16, 25; 6:8). In other words, our wills should be totally submitted to the will of the Spirit of the Lord. This will be worked out daily by obedience to His leading.

6. Prayer. A Christian who has no time to pray is like a man chopping a tree with a blunt axe. He won't stop to sharpen the axe because he wants to get the tree chopped down. Sharpening the axe for a few minutes will greatly speed up the job. Take time to sharpen your axe through prayer.

Remember that prayer is two-way communication between God and man. Take time to listen for God's encouragement, comfort, correction, and direction.

7. Know your enemy. Realize that you have a three-fold enemy—the world, the flesh, and the devil. If you "crucify" the flesh (your old sinful nature), the world will have no attraction for you, and the devil will have no foothold on you. Satan is the god of this world, the tempter, the "accuser of the brethren"—your enemy. Become familiar with Ephesians 6:10–20 and 1 Peter 5:8–10.

8. Saved to serve. If you know what you have been saved from, you will know what you have been saved for. Over 140,000 people die every twenty-four hours. Devote your life entirely to reaching them with the Gospel of salvation. There is no higher calling.

You Really Mean It?

Once you've led someone to the Lord and instructed him the basic principles of Christian living, you may never see that person again. This is especially true if he was a stranger or passer-by whom you met in a public place. While follow-up is important, it's not always possible. But you can take the new convert as far as he is ready to go at the time. Don't stop with the sinner's prayer if God leads you to go further.

Philip's encounter with the Ethiopian eunuch shows us how to make the most of a one-time opportunity.

When Philip ran up to the chariot of the Bible-reading Ethiopian eunuch, he knew he had an awakened sinner ripe for the picking. The eunuch said he didn't understand the prophetic words of Isaiah concerning the Messiah, so Philip hopped in the chariot, *"opened his mouth, and beginning at this Scripture, preached Jesus to him"* (Acts 8:35). As they continued down the road, they came to some water, and the eunuch said, *"See, here is water. What hinders me from being baptized?"* (v. 36).

Notice that Philip did not say, "A six-week training course!" He just answered, *"If you believe with all your heart, you may"* (v. 37). The eunuch answered, *"I believe that Jesus Christ is the Son of God"* (v. 37). Then Philip baptized him immediately.

Considering the massive backsliding rate within the church, I can understand why some are hesitant to baptize new converts. When the pastor looks through the baptismal records and finds that eight out of ten are slipping away, he has to do something! So he provides instruction courses on water baptism.

But those who drop all man-made methods of manipulation and work with the Holy Spirit will see sinners put their hand to the plow and never even look back. When sinners come through the door of conviction, they can, like the Philippian jailer and the Ethiopian eunuch, be baptized the same hour of the night. Our confidence must be in the keeping power of God—not in the binding control of human rules and regulations. If they're His sheep, they will follow Him. Your part is to lead them as far as they are ready to go at the time—the rest of the way they must depend on the Good Shepherd.

14

Who Are the Backsliders?

ave you ever felt guilty when a new convert has backslidden? Perhaps you said to yourself, "If only I had given him another trailer-load of follow-up! I should have encouraged him more, picked him up, and taken him to meetings."

Well, if you have said that, take consolation from our Ethiopian brother's conversion. After Philip explained the Scriptures, the Ethiopian eunuch believed and wanted to be baptized.

> Now when they came up out of the water, the Spirit of the Lord caught Philip away, so that the eunuch saw him no more; and he went on his way rejoicing. But Philip was found at Azotus. And passing through, he preached in all the cities till he came to Caesarea. (Acts 8:39–40)

Notice that Philip left the Ethiopian without follow-up. In fact, I am not totally correct in that statement—according to the last verse, *the Lord* left that new convert without follow-up.

A *genuine* conversion will stand no matter how great the adversity. *"Though he fall, he shall not be utterly cast down"*

(Psalm 37:24). *"Do not rejoice over me, my enemy; when I fall, I will arise"* (Micah 7:8).

Have you ever pondered why Jesus sent His lambs among wolves? (See Luke 10:3.) Surely that is contrary to our pampering and shielding of lambs! He knew that temptation, tribulation, and persecution would prove them! He knew that adversity would eventually expose the backslider in heart.

The backslider in heart is *"filled with his own ways"* (Proverbs 14:14), yet on the outside he appears to be full of God's ways. I have seen many of these conversions. These believers can be found with buttons, Jesus stickers, Christian T-shirts—everything except fruit! They are a reproach to the Gospel.

The True Test

Years ago I read in the local newspaper that a men's store had found a brown paper package outside their store one Monday morning. An accompanying note gave the explanation, "I stole these trousers from you on Friday, became a Christian on Sunday, and here they are on Monday. Please forgive me." That is fruit befitting repentance!

In the previous chapters we have looked at the need to use the Law of God as a "measuring rod" to show the sinner the *guilt* of his sin and thereby bring about true repentance. If the sinner has had *true* repentance and he is thereby "abiding in Christ," certain fruit should become evident:

> *Therefore, my brethren, you also have become dead to the law through the body of Christ...that we should bear fruit to God.* (Romans 7:4)

Remember our speedster? He was completely freed from the demands of the law by the sacrifice of his father. If he is *genuinely* sorrowful for his transgression, he will now show from a thankful heart the fruit of a new lifestyle. He will now desire to please his father in his every action.

Scripture says that *"the root of the righteous yields fruit"* (Proverbs 12:12). If we are rooted and grounded in Him, there should be evidence of certain fruit.

> *I am the vine, you are the branches. He who abides in Me, and I in him, bears **much fruit;** for without Me you can do nothing.* (John 15:5, emphasis added)

> *That you may walk worthy of the Lord, fully pleasing Him, being **fruitful in every good work.***
> (Colossians 1:10, emphasis added)

What do the Scriptures mean when they say "fruit"? Before we look at the answer, let's examine John the Baptist's response to certain Jews who came to the Jordan where he was baptizing.

> *But when he saw many of the Pharisees and Sadducees coming to his baptism, he said to them, "Brood of vipers! Who warned you to flee from the wrath to come? Therefore bear fruits worthy of repentance....And even now the ax is laid to the root of the trees. Therefore every tree which does not bear good fruit is cut down and thrown into the fire."* (Matthew 3:7–8, 10)

Another fruit of genuine repentance is the fruit of a thankful heart to God. The apostle Paul said, *"Thanks be to God for His indescribable gift"* (2 Corinthians 9:15).

Scripture also speaks of *"the fruit of our lips, giving thanks to His name"* (Hebrews 13:15).

Certain fruit should grow within our lives because of the presence of the Holy Spirit.

> *But the fruit of the Spirit is love, joy, peace, longsuf-fering, kindness, goodness, faithfulness, gentleness, self-control. Against such there is no law.*
> (Galatians 5:22–23)

And last but not least, everyone who names the name of Christ should depart from iniquity. Repentance is a per-petual turning from sin and being *"filled with the fruits of righteousness"* (Philippians 1:11).

What I am saying is this: *"**Every** tree which does not bear **good fruit** is cut down and **thrown into the fire**"* (Mat-thew 3:10, emphasis added). As witnesses of the Gospel, we must do everything we can to produce fruit-bearing commitments to Christ—not just "decisions" that result in church members, but commitments that result in *fruit bear-ers.*

The Stony-Ground Hearer

To gain insight into what produces and what hinders fruit, let's look at the Word of God. After Jesus told the mul-titudes the parable of the sower, His disciples questioned Him privately.

> *And He said to them, "Do you not understand this parable? How then will you understand all the para-bles? The sower sows the word. And these are the ones by the wayside where the word is sown. When they hear, Satan comes immediately and takes away*

*the word that was sown in their hearts. These like-
wise are the ones sown on stony ground who, when
they hear the word, immediately receive it with
gladness; and they have no root in themselves, and
so endure only for a time. Afterward, when tribulation or persecution arises for the word's sake,
immediately they stumble. Now these are the ones
sown among thorns; they are the ones who hear
the word, and the cares of this world, the deceitfulness of riches, and the desires for other things entering in choke the word, and it becomes unfruitful.
But these are the ones sown on good ground, those
who hear the word, accept it, and bear fruit: some
thirtyfold, some sixty, and some a hundred."*
(Mark 4:13–20)

The parable of the sower is also recorded in Matthew 13
and Luke 8. Using the harmony of the Gospels, let's look at
the six characteristics of the stony-ground hearer.

1. He responds immediately. (See Mark 4:5).
2. He lacks depth. (See Mark 4:5.)
3. He has no root. (See Matthew 13:6.)
4. He receives the word with gladness. (See Mark
4:16.)
5. He receives the word with joy. (See Matthew
13:20.)
6. He does believe for a while. (See Luke 8:13.)

Keep in mind that only God can see beneath the soil to
know what is going on in a man's heart. But God has given
us insight into what He sees by telling us to watch for certain
evidence that will reveal the condition of the soil.

When we see a plant with a strong stem and green
leaves, we conclude that all is well. Conversely, a scrawny

seedling may look like it's struggling for survival. But have you ever seen a plant that was seemingly healthy and later died?

When the sun beats down, the true condition of the plant becomes evident. What happens when the sun seems to be killing a larger plant and benefiting a smaller one? The stronger-looking plant may have an inadequate root system for the rocky soil in which it's planted. Nutrients may be sent into the leaves and stem instead of going into the roots. The scrawny plant may actually have an extensive root system that helps it survive heat and drought.

Can you see that the sun is responsible for revealing the discrepancy under the soil? In the spiritual realm the sun is said to be:

1. Tribulation. (See Matthew 13:21.)
2. Temptation. (See Luke 8:13.)
3. Persecution. (See Mark 4:17.)

These three factors reveal what we cannot see—the condition of the sinner's heart.

Grow or Die!

If we want a plant to produce fruit, we must expose it to sunlight. Placing a plant in a dimly lit area stunts its growth. In the same way, we need not fear the sunlight of tribulation, temptation, and persecution coming to a new convert. They will prove him! If he is genuine in his commitment, he will grow; if his heart is not right, he will wither and die.

I once heard a story about two Russian guards who burst into a prayer meeting in the Soviet Union. They pointed their machine guns at twenty people who had gathered for the meeting and said, "If you are not prepared to die for your faith, get out now!" Immediately a number left. The guards then put down their guns and said, "Praise the Lord! We thought we'd sort out the sheep from the goats before we'd risk fellowship."

Our churches need a "Russian guard clean-out." Such a purge in our twentieth century church would have a two-fold effect:

First, persecution would uproot "tares" from the church. Those who cause division, those who quench the Spirit, those with hearts of unbelief, and those who continually murmur and complain would leave. God didn't use the "Russian guard" method in the Old Testament. He used the "ground opening up and swallowing them" method.

Second, and what's more important, the stony-ground hearer would see the error of his ways! Can you imagine the tragedy of propping up a stony-ground hearer until Judgment Day, when he comes under the ultimate sunlight of God's wrath? Imagine if you are responsible for shielding him from the sunlight. By letting him fall now, he has the opportunity to get his heart right before God.

For years I spent my energy asking stony-ground hearers, "Are you reading the Word?" My heart sank at disappointing answers like, "I've been busy," "I've been tired," or "Now and then." A healthy lamb has a healthy appetite. He disciplines himself to read and feed upon the Bible. He sees the Bible as a love letter to himself and meditates on the Word both day and night.

A number of years ago I talked with a young man about his Christian walk. Richard expressed concern that he didn't measure up to what he knew a Christian should be.

I asked him what evidence he had that he was a Christian. I asked him if he had the love spoken of in Scripture; he answered "no." I asked him if he had joy; again he gave negative response. As I named each of those nine fruits of the Spirit, he admitted that he didn't possess any of them.

I looked Richard in the eye and said, "Richard, upon your own confession, I see no evidence that you are a Christian." Some time later he told me that my response angered him. Nevertheless, he went home, examined himself to see if he was in the faith, concluded that he wasn't, and repented with all his heart. Within three months Richard was in a responsible position within the church because he was such a fruit bearer!

Ready to Be Used?

The cares of the world, the deceitfulness of riches, and the desire for other things have a continual pull on the affections of the stony-ground hearer. Yet Jesus said that if convert even looks back, something is wrong:

> But Jesus said to him, "No one, having put his hand
> to the plow, and looking back, is fit for the kingdom
> of God."   (Luke 9:62)

The word *"fit"* comes from a Greek word, *eutheto*, which means "ready to use."

Not everyone mentioned in the New Testament was read to be used by God. Look closely at the following portion of Scripture and notice how the apostle Paul failed to put a "seal of approval" upon his fellow laborer, Demas.

> Tychicus, a beloved brother, faithful minister, and
> fellow servant in the Lord, will tell you all the news

about me....With Onesimus, a faithful and beloved brother, who is one of you....Aristarchus my fellow prisoner greets you, with Mark the cousin of Barnabas (about whom you received instructions: if he comes to you, welcome him)....These are my only fellow workers for the kingdom of God who are of the circumcision; they have proved to be a comfort to me. Epaphras, who is one of you, a bondservant of Christ, greets you, always laboring fervently for you in prayers, that you may stand perfect and complete in all the will of God....Luke the beloved physician and Demas greet you.

(Colossians 4:7, 9–12, 14)

The apostle Paul referred to other workers as "faithful," "beloved," "one of you," or "servants of Christ," but at Demas' name he was obviously silent. Paul refrained from putting a stamp of approval on Demas. He did not say "receive him." We can see why by turning to another one of Paul's epistles: *"For Demas has forsaken me, having loved this present world"* (2 Timothy 4:10).

The sunlight of temptation had finally exposed the condition of his heart. He had loved the world more than God. *"If anyone loves the world, the love of the Father is not in him"* (1 John 2:15). Having put his hand to the plow and looked back, he wasn't fit for the kingdom of God.

Don't Waste Your Time

When the Bible says, *"Walk in wisdom toward those who are outside, redeeming the time"* (Colossians 4:5), it doesn't just mean those who are "outside" your particular church. Scripture is talking about those who are outside the body of Christ. Stony-ground hearers are outside; if we desire to redeem the time, we need to walk in wisdom toward them.

At least twice, the apostle Paul warned of false brethren. False brethren are often the instruments satan uses to wear out the saints. I have, in the past, literally spent hours counseling people who didn't need counsel—they needed repentance! All the fertilizer in the world won't help a plant with a faulty root system.

Jesus wasn't always available. In fact, He often hid from people because He knew their hearts. (See Mark 7:24; John 11:54.) These people don't want your words; they just want your time. You cast your pearls of godly wisdom, and they trample them underfoot. They are hearers of the Word and not doers.

How much better for us to put our energies into the unsaved! We need to walk in wisdom, redeem the time, and put our efforts into reaching this world with the Gospel while it is day, for the night is coming, when no man can work.

15

Success Comes in "Cans"

I believe that one of the greatest encumbrances of evangelism today is that multitudes of "set free," "Spirit-filled," "Bible believing" Christians are bound by an inferiority complex. They are paralyzed by the fear of man.

For years I suffered from an inferiority complex. I was called "Red Indian" in elementary school because I blushed. On becoming a Christian I was totally set free. What was the key to my deliverance? I saw that inferiority and shyness are just a subtle form of pride. We fear what people will think of us! "They will look at me. I will make a fool of myself."

When I sought the Lord as to why I used to feel so inferior, He reminded me of a hurtful experience that happened when I was nine years old. For something to do, a group of boys took me to the school football field, held my arms, and proceeded to kick a football at me—just for fun.

Just recently I realized what a scar that incident had left on me. My voice used to crack with emotion as I related that incident to other Christians. My peers had probably picked on me because I was only a small fellow who could put up little resistance. The experience had left me with a terrible sense of rejection! "What was wrong with me? Why don't they like me? Why can't they accept me?"

Whatever the cause of our feelings of rejection, we must forget it when we come to Christ! We must forget for the Gospel's sake. The Bible says that *"old things have passed away"* (2 Corinthians 5:17). We should continually be *"forgetting those things which are behind"* (Philippians 3:13).

Yet multitudes of Christians are paralyzed in their pews, desiring to be free in Christ, not realizing that the answer is in their hands—they hold the keys to their own prison.

Psychology tells us, "You will become what you imagine yourself to be." In other words, if you continually say to yourself, "I could never speak up for the Gospel. I'm too shy. I could never do that," that is what you will eventually become. Even the Scriptures affirm, *"For as he thinks in his heart, so is he"* (Proverbs 23:7).

A Christian with a defeated mental confession undermines the work of Calvary. Jesus died to set you free from the works of the devil! He opened to you the power of heaven. You can begin to think differently because the almighty Creator of the universe is with you.

Renew your mind and begin confessing what you are in Christ. With faith in your heart, you can start making the following biblical confessions:

> *I can do all things through Christ who strengthens me.* (Philippians 4:13)
>
> *If God is for* [me], *who can be against* [me]? (Romans 8:31)

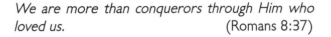

We are more than conquerors through Him who loved us. (Romans 8:37)

He who is in [me] is greater than he who is in the world. (1 John 4:4)

See yourself as being mighty in God. Forget about yourself, your lack of height, your big nose, and your blushing. Forget about past rejection and failures; you are a new creature in Jesus Christ. All those past events have become non-issues.

The world needs to be reached with the Gospel, and you are needed as a soldier in the army of the Lord. You can have the greatest privilege a man or woman can have in this world—you can minister eternal life to dying humanity.

Kick with All Your Heart

Two frogs jumped into a bowl of cream and got stuck. One said to himself, "How did I ever get into this bowl of cream? I just can't seem to get out, so I might as well sink back down and drown. Besides, there are plenty of worse ways for a frog to die—I could be torn to pieces by a cat! Yes, that's what I'll do—I'll just sink down in this cream and drown."

The second frog said to himself, "No way will I croak in a bowl of cream! I refuse to die easily—I'm going to fight this with all my strength! If I do go down, I'm going down with flags flying!"

He began to kick, splash, and flap his little flippers. He would not give up! Every ounce of energy was put into kicking against that cream, until a strange thing happened. That cream thickened because of his constant kicking, until finally it turned to butter, and he leaped out of it!

The first frog died of an inferiority complex. The second was in the same bowl of cream, but his attitude was different. As you begin to kick out at that particular "cream," whatever it may be, by God's grace, that weakness will eventually be conquered, and you will leap out of it with great rejoicing.

Remember, the attitude you have about your particular problem will determine your victory. Do you really want to be free? Do you really want to be used by God? Do you really care about the unsaved? If so, begin kicking with all your heart.

Shake Off the Hindrances

While I was seeking God concerning my inferiority complex, I came across the following passage:

Now when they had escaped, they then found out that the island was called Malta. And the natives showed us unusual kindness; for they kindled a fire and made us all welcome, because of the rain that was falling and because of the cold. But when Paul had gathered a bundle of sticks and laid them on the fire, a viper came out because of the heat, and fastened on his hand. So when the natives saw the creature hanging from his hand, they said to one another, "No doubt this man is a murderer, whom, though he has escaped the sea, yet justice does not allow to live." But he shook off the creature into the fire and suffered no harm. However, they were expecting that he would swell up or suddenly fall down dead. But after they had looked for a long time and saw no harm come to him, they changed their minds and said that he was a god.

(Acts 28:1–6)

The same day I sought the Lord for a reason for my complex, I saw this passage in a new light. A venomous beast seeks to hang on to the hand of every Christian. The "hand" of the Christian is the area of his effectiveness in God.

That old serpent, the devil, seeks to sink his teeth into your area of effectiveness, pour in his venom, and totally paralyze your ministry! His venom is indeed poison: bitterness, resentment, jealousy, inferiority, pride, accusations, and condemnation!

Notice the apostle Paul's reaction to his plight. He did not say, "There seems to be a venomous beast clinging to my hand. I will ask God for a miracle—perhaps a small bolt of lightning would remove it from my hand." Nor did he say to himself, "Ten out of ten die with this type of snake bite! I'll just lie down here and die."

No way! *"But he shook off the creature into the fire and suffered no harm"* (Acts 28:5). Can you see the two keys to his deliverance? First, Paul did the shaking. God expects you to do something about your condition. You lay aside that weight! You put off the old man with its deeds. Change your attitude, and begin to kick with all your might.

Second, Paul held the beast over the fire. The shaking and the heat loosened the snake from his hand. Satan will flee from you if you will let the fire of God consume you!

Get Out of My Way!

During one of my pre-dawn prayer walks, I came across some cows in the middle of the road blocking my path. As I approached them, I said, "I believe that God has put the fear of me in you. Now get out of my way!" Just as I said that, I noticed that these "cows" didn't have udders, and one had horns. But before I could run, they parted like the Red Sea.

What beast stands in your path? Is it the ugly beast of the fear of man, the fear of failure, or unbelief? Whatever it may be, tell it to get out of your way! Remember the words of Scripture: *"You will also declare a thing, and it will be established for you"* (Job 22:28).

If God is for you, *nothing* can be against you. If that "beast" won't get out of the way, stomp on it! Tread on the scorpion, and crush the snake with your heel!

If only we could catch a glimpse of the authority we have in prayer. Sue and I often sit on our patio, enjoying the warmth of the sun. Some time ago, one of our neighbors planted a tree that, in a few years, would have grown up and blocked our sunlight. I was sure our neighbor would have been offended if I asked him to move the tree, so I cursed it in the name of Jesus. It withered and died! Now my neighbor is cursing the tree and not me.

Dear Christian, you, too, can do it! God's Word promises that you will see results from faith-filled, authoritative prayer in the name of Jesus. You are an ambassador for Christ. You have power with God. You can boldly come before the throne of grace and through prayer govern the destiny of nations.

Often when I do things for God, I am petrified, but if I care enough for the cause, I will ignore my fear. Be consoled by knowing that I am also riddled with a thousand other weaknesses. But God helps me to *"walk in the Spirit"* so that I won't *"fulfill the lust of the flesh"* (Galatians 5:16).

My frailties keep me on my face before the Lord and confirm Paul's revelation, *"When I am weak, **then** I am strong"* (2 Corinthians 12:10, emphasis added). Don't let anything stop your burning for God. Burn in Bible study, in prayer, and in your zeal to evangelize. Burn so that only charred ashes of the flesh remain.

Baptized with Fire

Do you think John the Baptist had an inferiority complex? He had no fear of man! He reproved Herod for his adulterous relationship; he called the Pharisees a brood of vipers. He was not afraid of man because the fire of God burned within his bones! He was filled with the Holy Spirit to overflowing.

John said of Jesus, *"He will baptize you with the Holy Spirit and with fire"* (Luke 3:16). Everywhere I go I find Christians baptized with the Holy Spirit but not with the fire!

Those with the fire of God within them don't even notice if they blush! They don't notice their inadequacies. They have shaken off resentment, pride, bitterness, and other subtle hindrances to the work they must do for God. The zeal of God's house has consumed them. They love God more than their own pleasures, and they fear God more than man. They cannot but speak that which they have seen and heard! They are overcomers because *"they did not love their lives to the death"* (Revelation 12:11).

I was reading recently about a well-to-do lady in New York who decided to throw a banquet for her friends. While she was waiting for the meal, the chief cook called her into the kitchen. The cook had been given some mushrooms that she suspected could be toadstools. The woman suggested they experiment on the old dog who sat just outside the kitchen door. The dog was subsequently given the mushrooms and watched for thirty minutes. He had no adverse reaction, so the mushrooms were thrown in the cooking pot.

During the meal a pale-faced cook approached the host and whispered that the dog had just died. The woman decided that the ethical thing to do was to tell her guests the whole story. As soon as she mentioned that the dog had just died, some of her guests clutched their stomachs in pain, another bent double. Others felt quite sick while two went off to call an ambulance.

The hostess thought it strange that she had eaten the same meal and yet had no ill effects, so she decided to take a look at the dead dog. When she asked the cook where the dog was, the reply came, "Oh, I wouldn't look at him if I were you—the truck that hit him left him in a terrible mess!" After hearing the true fate of the dog, the guests made a remarkable recovery.

The truth of the matter is, if you keep believing the lies of the devil, you will eventually develop the symptoms! What you must do is stop believing the lie and begin proclaiming the truth!

Change Your Confession

Jeremiah suffered from an inferiority complex. When the mighty God of Israel ordained him to be a prophet to the nations, Jeremiah said, *"Ah, Lord GOD! Behold, I cannot speak, for I am a youth"* (Jeremiah 1:6). Notice the Lord's response to the reluctant prophet: *"But the LORD said to me: 'Do not say, "I am a youth"'"* (v. 7). God told him to change his confession!

God told Jeremiah, *"Do not say, 'I am a youth,'"* because it wasn't true! The truth is "I am more than a conqueror, I can do all things through Christ....I am a giant in God....If God be for me, nothing can be against me!"

Find a place where you can confess the truth verbally. Don't just think it; say it—shout it! Then keep saying it until it moves from your head to your heart! "Goliath of inferiority, watch out; I'm going to take the two-edged sword, cut off your head, then stand upon you in triumph!"

Let's return to the passage in Jeremiah.

> *"Do not be afraid of their faces, for I am with you to deliver you," says the LORD. Then the LORD put forth His hand and touched my mouth, and the LORD said to me: "Behold, I have put My words in your mouth."*
> (Jeremiah 1:8–9)

God put His words in Jeremiah's mouth. Let the Word of God dwell richly within your heart. When you speak it out, you are using the creative force. I have heard demons scream when the Word of God is confessed. Confess it with faith in your heart. "No weapon formed against me shall prosper!" (See Isaiah 54:17.) No venom that satan seeks to pump into me will penetrate!

Then what did God instruct Jeremiah to do?

> *Therefore prepare yourself and arise, and speak to*
> *them all that I command you. Do not be dismayed*
> *before their faces, lest I dismay you before them.*
>
> (Jeremiah 1:17)

What the Lord is saying is, "Get it together, Jeremiah, because if you are disobedient, I will make you look like a fool in front of them!"

To be fearful of man is to lack faith in God. Remember, to lack faith in God when He says He will be with us is to say, "God, You're a liar!" If we feared God, we wouldn't dare think such a thing. If we feared God, we wouldn't fear man. God has not given us a cringing spirit of fear, but a spirit of power, of love, and of a sound mind. (See 2 Timothy 1:7.)

Let's look at Jeremiah a few chapters later.

> *Then I said, "I will not make mention of Him, nor*
> *speak anymore in His name." But His word was in*
> *my heart like a burning fire shut up in my bones; I*
> *was weary of holding it back, and I could not.*
>
> (Jeremiah 20:9)

Praise God, look at the difference after God put His Word in Jeremiah's mouth! When Jeremiah was called, he could not speak; after he obeyed God and let the fire of God consume him, he could not keep quiet! That should be the testimony of every Christian! Every believer should be on fire for God. Every Christian should have the fire of God burning in his bones!

Brother or sister, if you aren't consumed with the zeal of God, ask the Holy Spirit to stir the depths of your soul.

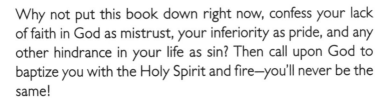

Why not put this book down right now, confess your lack of faith in God as mistrust, your inferiority as pride, and any other hindrance in your life as sin? Then call upon God to baptize you with the Holy Spirit and fire—you'll never be the same!

What Motivates You?

A motive is a conscious or unconscious need or drive. We can have a motive for doing or not doing something, and not even be aware of that motive.

The following question can reveal a hidden motive for the "fear of man": If someone gave you $1,000 for every person you witnessed to, would you become more zealous in your evangelism? I remember thinking deeply about the question for one or two seconds. I came to the conclusion that if that were the case, I would begin 4:00 A.M. "flashlight evangelism."

Think about it for a moment. Could you deal with your own "fear of man" problem for money? Would we serve mammon with more zeal than God? I found that my priorities were still wrong. I preferred the praise of men to the praise of God. I was not a "living sacrifice." A good dose of repentance was what the doctor ordered. Why grasp the key of knowledge if we are not willing to use it?

God has not only given us promises, but He has also given us His Spirit to help us in our weaknesses. To believe that you can be an effective soulwinner is merely to believe those promises.

A pastor once asked me to do a series of meetings, adding, "I'll get back to you after you've had a chance to pray about it." Without wanting to sound presumptuous, I said,

"No need to. I've been praying for God to open doors, and when one opens I'm coming through—I'd love to minister!" The pastor smiled and said, "Now that's real trust!"

But some may say, "Ah—it could be the devil!" Well, if it is, he's answering my prayer. I want doors to open so that I can preach God's Word, see saints set on fire, and sinners soundly saved. God is faithful to hear and answer when our motives are centered on doing His will.

Order your priorities. Let compassion swallow your fears, and let the fear of the Lord be your servant and the Law of God your sickle.

Let me tell you a true but tragic story. A woman was once walking along a riverbank with her child. Suddenly the child slipped into the river. The mother screamed in terror. She couldn't swim, and besides, she was in the latter stages of pregnancy. Finally, somebody heard her screaming and rushed down to the riverbank. The utter tragedy was, when they stepped into those murky waters to retrieve that now dead child, they found that the water was only waist deep! That mother could have easily saved her child but didn't because of a lack of knowledge.

Listen carefully. Satan would have you stand paralyzed on the riverbank of the fear of man, believing that the waters of personal evangelism are too deep for you. But let knowledge release you. As you step out into those murky waters of personal witness, your feet will stand firmly upon the sure and true promises of almighty God. He will not let you down.

You Can Reach the Lost

One day I turned on a radio to hear that a certain airline was offering reduced rates to Hawaii. Excitement gripped me at the thought of preaching there, so I mentioned it to my wife, Sue. While studying Scripture that day she had read, "Go and possess the land of the palm trees," so we booked our tickets in faith.

We arrived at Honolulu Airport with promise of ministry but no accommodations. We had seen in travel brochures that the cost of living in Hawaii was extremely expensive—up to $300 per night for an apartment! So we hoped that somehow, someone, somewhere would house us.

The Scripture on my heart was that Abraham went north, not knowing where he was going. I remember thinking that we also might be dwelling in tents as Abraham did.

From the airport I telephoned the group I was scheduled to minister with. They said they hadn't found living quarters for us but had instead booked us into a luxury apartment! On arrival, we found that it was fully furnished, with two bedrooms, cooking facilities, radio, TV, private swimming pool, spa, and tennis courts. With fear and trembling, I asked about the price. The total cost per night was eighteen dollars!

A church organization owned this whole block of apartments, and this was one of two set aside for missionaries and traveling preachers. We were told that we were very "lucky" as there had been a cancellation two days before we arrived.

Claim these exceeding great and precious promises found in God's Word. Boldly say, *"The LORD is my helper; I will not fear. What can man do to me?"* (Hebrews 13:6). With the Law of God on one hand, and the promises of God on the

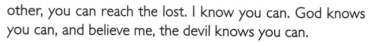

other, you can reach the lost. I know you can. God knows you can, and believe me, the devil knows you can.

What you must do is know that *you can,* yourself. Like Joshua of old, you can have "good success." You "can do all things through Christ who strengthens you" if you will only believe you can. Remember—success comes in "cans."

16

You've Got What It Takes

The historian and philosopher, David Hume, was hurrying along the streets of London when a friend asked him where he was going. Hume replied that he was going to hear George Whitefield preach. The friend, knowing that Hume was none too friendly to Christianity, replied, "Surely you don't believe what Whitefield is preaching, do you?" "No," replied Hume, "but *he* does!"

Whether we are witnessing one-on-one or preaching to vast crowds, we must have a *genuine* enthusiasm—a fervency so great that our hearers will see we have strong convictions about what we are saying. John Wesley said, "Get on fire for God, and people will come to watch you burn!"

A preacher was once asked what was the best way to keep a congregation awake on a hot Sunday night. His reply was thought-provoking—"Have a deacon take a sharp stick and *prod the preacher!*" If the preacher is alive, the people will listen.

How can we get on fire and be used by God to win the lost? Let's now look at three key elements that are absolutely necessary for effective evangelism:

1. Faith

2. Love
3. Righteousness

Any Christian can use these three sticks to prod himself into a greater enthusiasm in sharing his faith.

The first stick with which we should keep ourselves prodded is the stick of *faith*. With faith we can please God, but *"without faith it is impossible to please Him"* (Hebrews 11:6). Faith in the spiritual realm is what oxygen is to the natural realm.

A few years ago I was interested in making a Christian movie that would cost thousands of dollars. To help offset the cost, I applied to a trust fund for a substantial amount of money. When six months had passed, I wondered if they had forgotten me.

Late one Friday afternoon, I couldn't wait any longer. I telephoned the trust fund and asked if they had granted the money. The person at the other end left the phone, checked the records, and responded, "You've got what you applied for—thirty-five hundred dollars."

I thanked him, gently replaced the receiver, then jumped for sheer joy while shouting, "I got it!" I danced, laughed, and even hugged a somewhat bewildered friend who was in our home at the time. I didn't care what others thought of me—I was celebrating the fact that the money was finally mine.

Let's look at this situation objectively. Why was I excited? I didn't actually have one cent of that money. All I really had was a promise! That man on the phone had said that the money was coming, and I had believed him.

Can you see that faith in his word gave me joy, and that joy had actually been a tremendous source of energy to me?

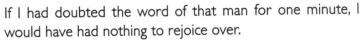

If I had doubted the word of that man for one minute, I would have had nothing to rejoice over.

But through faith I actually considered that money to be as good as being in my hand. Faith caused me to rejoice. Through the joy I had in believing, I felt renewed and tremendously energized! Faith had produced joy, and joy had produced energy.

No Faith—No Joy

If we can muster up faith in humanity, how much more should we have faith in God? As we believe the promises of God, we will begin to manifest *"joy unspeakable"* (1 Peter 1:8 KJV). Scripture also says that we will have *"all joy and peace in believing"* (Romans 15:13). That joy will result in greater energy in our witness.

In fact, all our joy should issue from objectivity rather than subjectivity. We shouldn't rely on energy produced from the joys of this life. If our zeal is produced from temporal victories, it won't be long until trials bum us out.

The apostle Paul and Silas rejoiced while sitting in a cold dungeon. No doubt they suffered tremendous pain from their whippings, yet they praised God at midnight. (See Acts 16:23–25.) They rejoiced because of the eternal, unchanging promises of God.

Jesus told His disciples, *"Nevertheless do not rejoice in this, that the spirits are subject to you, but rather rejoice because your names are written in heaven"* (Luke 10:20). If we make heaven the object of our rejoicing, we will keep our joy no matter what the circumstances on earth. We will always abound in the work of the Lord, knowing that our *"labor is not in vain in the Lord"* (1 Corinthians 15:58).

Someone once said that I was a man of great faith in God. This brother intended to compliment me, but actually it was nothing of the sort. The assertion, "I have great faith in my doctor," obviously compliments my doctor, not me.

A devious criminal could have great faith in my doctor. All the criminal needs to do is catch a glimpse of his character, reputation, and skill. In the same way, the most miserable of sinners can be a man of great faith in God.

The more faith I have, the more I give glory to God. That's what Abraham did.

> He did not waver at the promise of God through unbelief, but was strengthened in faith, giving glory to God, and being fully convinced that what He had promised He was able also to perform.
>
> (Romans 4:20–21)

You and I have no excuse for lacking faith in God. In fact, the amount of faith we have in Him will be evidenced by the energy we have for the kingdom of God. How much fire do you have in your bones? No fire, no joy; no joy, no faith; no faith, no salvation, for *"without faith it is impossible to please Him"* (Hebrews 11:6).

Joyless Christian, get on your knees and repent before the God you have insulted with your unbelief. Your lack of faith in God means that you think that He's not worth trusting. *"He who does not believe God has made Him a liar"* (1 John 5:10).

Perfect Love

Do you remember our speedster? If he truly saw the cost of the father's sacrifice, he would delight to do his father's will. When we catch a glimpse of the cost of Calvary and the love behind that cross, we grope for words to express gratitude. Service then becomes an expression of gratitude for the unspeakable gift. Our hearts cry, "O God, if You love me that much, I will do anything for You!"

Such love for God will cause you to cast your own fears behind your back. The love of Christ will cause you to do things you never thought possible. You will venture where others fear to tread because _"perfect love casts out fear"_ (1 John 4:18).

Some years ago, this truth became evident to me during a disturbance in our church foyer. A fairly large non-Christian was rather irate because his girlfriend had become a Christian and left his belongings on her front doorstep. No more fornication. When she came out of the meeting, he immediately punched her with both fists on her upper chest. I stepped between them. He then brought his fist back to deal with me. (A fly swatter would have been adequate.)

My wife, who stands just under five feet tall, pushed him and said, "Don't you touch my husband!" In frustration, he turned and thumped his fist against the wall, then stormed out of the door. My wife's perfect (mature) love had cast out all her fear. (She did begin to shake after the incident.)

In the same way, any fear you have, whether it be of darkness, of heights, of man, or of death, will be cast out if your love for God is mature. The apostle Paul's love for God was evident in his zeal to obey the Lord. Despite being told that bonds and afflictions awaited him in Jerusalem, he steadfastly forged ahead to fulfill his purpose.

But none of these things move me; nor do I count my life dear to myself, so that I may finish my race with joy, and the ministry which I received from the Lord Jesus, to testify to the gospel of the grace of God. (Acts 20:24)

Seeing the cross will cause us to extend our souls to the hungry and satisfy the afflicted soul. (See Isaiah 58:10.) We will have compassion on those around us, for we cannot love God and not love our neighbor.

Compassion comes from a compound Latin word (*com*—"with," *pati*—"suffer"). In other words, "to suffer with." A compassionate person can enter into another person's suffering, desiring to help. He is capable of empathy.

We hear much criticism of the church but comparatively little criticism of Christ. If we want to reach this world for God, we must exercise the love and compassion of Jesus. Love is our most powerful weapon.

I once gave an enthusiastic wave to a Christian brother. Unknown to me, another man was standing between us and was overwhelmed by my enthusiasm. He thought my wave was to him, and he came rushing across to meet me. Someone once said, "When love is felt, the message is heard." The simplest man with passion is more persuasive than the most eloquent without it.

Getting Our Hands Dirty

A lady dressed in silks and satins was standing on the curb of a Paris street when, to her horror, a ring with a very valuable jewel dropped from her finger into the filth of the gutter. She stooped instantly. With the bent handle of her elegant umbrella, she searched the gutter for it but could not find it. Then, as the astonished crowd looked on, she slipped the glove from her dainty white hand and, with her delicate fingers, searched through the water and mud until she found the lost jewel.

Are we prepared to search through the mud and get our hands dirty for the kingdom of God? Do we see alcoholics, drug addicts, and prostitutes through the eyes of love and faith as potential "trophies of grace"?

If the love of God dwells within our hearts, we will strip off formalism and begin to search the gutters of society for the lost gems of humanity as God searched for us. (See Malachi 3:17.) If the fields are white unto harvest, we need to get out of the barns and into those fields.

God has given us the key to bring conviction to the heart of the sinner, and once he is convicted we can, with the help of God, convert him. Many of us have the philosophy of "Go ye into the world and get a sinner to come to church so that the pastor can preach the Gospel to him."

The church should be a pulsating, dynamic, explosive, mighty army of dedicated soldiers who have gathered to feed the troops and check its weaponry. Once fed, we must go out into the dying world, preach, and live the Word—be salt and light. Jesus mixed with prostitutes and tax collectors, and yet He remained untainted by their sins.

I once saw a well-known pastor sitting right in the middle of a crowd of hardened sinners. On inquiry, he told me that he was almost "drying up" because of his constant fellowship with Christians and only Christians. He had come out to remind himself of the world, to hear rough talk, to mix with sinners before he matured into stagnation.

Righteousness Produces Confidence

If we want to hang on to zeal, we must continually work at it. God is interested in individuals. When Jesus had compassion on the multitude, it was because the multitude was made up of individuals.

Our love relationship with the Lord is like a good marriage. A thriving marriage happens only because both partners are working at it. Good relationships are founded upon communication, mutual respect, humility, and understanding. In the same way, we need to both communicate with God in prayer and listen to His voice through His Word and Spirit. We need to let the light of the Word search our hearts for hidden sin.

We have already looked at how faith produces energy, but righteousness will also produce zeal for God. Scripture, speaking of Christ, says, *"You have loved righteousness and hated lawlessness; therefore God, Your God, has anointed You with the oil of gladness more than Your companions"* (Hebrews 1:9). That same oil of gladness can be ours as we love righteousness and hate iniquity; that gladness will produce energy for the kingdom of God.

Righteousness produces a clear conscience so that we can boldly and confidently come before the throne of grace. Righteousness causes our relationship with the righteous Lord to blossom. Believers in right standing with God press on to know Him. Praise God that *"the people who know their God shall be strong, and carry out great exploits"* (Daniel 11:32).

There are only two occasions we should preach the Word: *"in season and out of season"* (2 Timothy 4:2). The

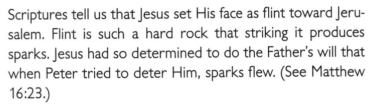
Scriptures tell us that Jesus set His face as flint toward Jerusalem. Flint is such a hard rock that striking it produces sparks. Jesus had so determined to do the Father's will that when Peter tried to deter Him, sparks flew. (See Matthew 16:23.)

Our love for God and for the lost should so burn within us that we set our faces as flint to do the will of God! Nothing should deter us from fulfilling the ministry we have received from Him.

The world will see our zeal as fanaticism, but we will endure misunderstanding, despising the shame, for our eyes are set upon Jesus. Allow the fire in your heart to be kindled by those incredible words of commendation, *"Well done, good and faithful servant"* (Matthew 25:21).

The Business of the Church

The supreme business of the church is to carry out Christ's Great Commission to preach the Gospel and make disciples of every nation. Jesus encouraged His disciples to pray to the Lord of the harvest, asking Him to thrust laborers into the whitened fields. (See Matthew 9:37–38.)

God's will is for all men to be saved and come to a knowledge of the truth. (See 1 Timothy 2:4.) The fallen nature of man, however, resists doing the will of God. A great wrestling match between the forces of hell and the drawing power of God is being waged for each sinner.

Multitudes of sinners are in the valley of decision. If they only knew the issues, they would seek salvation. Unbelief clouds their minds as they sit in darkened ignorance in the valley of the shadow of death.

With the spiritual authority given to the church, we must break the demonic powers that blind the minds of the unbelieving. Let us pray fervently for opportunities and boldness to bring them the light of the Gospel.

David Brainerd, the well-known missionary to the American Indians who literally poured his soul out unto death, was renowned for his prayer life. This only existed because he had a heart after God and after the souls of men. Look at his burden:

> I cared not where or how I lived, or what hardships I went through, so that I could but gain souls to Christ....O that I were a flaming torch in the hands of God.

Matthew Henry, the famous Bible commentator, did not wane in zeal for the lost behind the dry dust of theology. This soulwinner said, "I would think it a greater happiness to gain one soul to Christ than mountains of silver and gold to myself."

Another genius of Bible expositors, literary wit, and master of words, Charles Haddon Spurgeon, never lost sight of the point of the spearhead of the Gospel:

> I have no confidence at all in polished speech or brilliant literary effort to bring about a revival, but I have all the confidence in the world in the poor saint who would weep her eyes out because people are living in sin. I would choose, if I might, under God, to be a soulwinner.

You can be an effective witness for God. Don't let anything stand in your way. You may never know how sharing your faith with one person can affect an entire family, city, or nation. Think of those who had the privilege of influenc-ing D. L. Moody or Charles Finney for Christ!

During one of my early morning prayer walks, as the sun rose directly behind me, I was delighted to notice that my shadow was at least fifty feet long. The Lord spoke to my heart, and I want to share this word with you. "Remain small in your own eyes, walk the path of righteousness and faithful servitude, and you will find that the risen Son of Righteous-ness will extend the shadow of your ministry beyond your wildest dreams." You and I have what it takes to be success-ful soulwinners for God.

Developing Discipline

God has given us the tools, but it's up to us to develop the discipline and determination to use them.

I once took an eager Christian brother with me to do a series of meetings. We were given a double room to stay in and both set our alarms to go off around 5:45 A.M. for a time of prayer. I knew that his watch was a little fast so, wanting to be ahead of time, I set mine to go off a minute or so before his.

At 5:42 my watch woke me, but I noticed something dif-ferent in its sound. To my amazement, both watches were sounding their alarms in exact unison. In fact, the "beep beep" noises were so in step that I had difficulty distinguish-ing two alarms—they sounded like one.

I really don't know if I should attribute the incident to coincidence or to God. But one thing I do know, God is put-ting an alarm in the hearts of Christians to awake and pray in unison with each other and with His will. He is looking for men and women who will cry out, *"Spare Your people,*

O Lord, and do not give Your heritage to reproach" (Joel 2:17).

Perhaps you find it difficult to arise in the early hours to pray. Scripture says of Jesus, *"Now in the morning, having risen a long while before daylight, He went out and departed to a solitary place; and there He prayed"* (Mark 1:35).

Most nights, I get up for a time of prayer in the early hours of the morning. This isn't "super-spiritual"; I am able to do this because of my lifestyle. If it tires me, I take a nap during the day.

One Friday night, as Sue and I got into bed, I said, "Tonight I am not getting up to pray. I have ministry this weekend, so I'm sleeping right through!" That night around midnight, for no reason at all, our double bed collapsed! We had slept in it over five thousand times without incident. Needless to say, I had a very memorable time of prayer that night.

The problem with most of us bedridden believers is that we become involved in "the battle of the blanket." What's more, we surrender without putting up too much of a fight. If that is your experience, do what I do—take the blanket captive. I get up in the middle of the night, wrap myself in a large blanket, and pray.

All it takes is discipline and a change of lifestyle. Go to bed at 8:30 P.M. If such an early hour is unattractive, get up at 5:30 A.M. for a few mornings, and you will gladly hit the sack at 8:30 P.M.

A. W. Tozer's wise words may be applied to prayer as well as salvation: "The impulse to pursue God originates with God." If you don't have a desire to pray, ask God to give it to you.

Help in Prayer

A champion weight lifter whom I knew had given his life to Christ and came to our home for prayer for the baptism in the Holy Spirit. As he walked in front of me through our small home, I remember thinking that his massive back looked like the front wall of a squash court. His upper arms were easily the size of my thighs.

As we knelt on the carpet of the living room, I told him to raise his arms in worship and expect God to touch him as we prayed. After a few minutes, I opened my eyes and was encouraged to see both his arms shaking under the anointing. His facial expression was intense, and sweat was pouring from his brow. I leaned forward and whispered, "Getting a touch from the Lord, brother?" To this he replied, "No, my arms—they're so heavy!"

If your arms are heavy, your knees are feeble, the heavens seem as brass, and daily trials weigh upon you, then take heed to these words: *"Strengthen the hands which hang down, and the feeble knees, and make straight paths for your feet"* (Hebrews 12:12–13).

Sometimes I find that the heavens seem as brass. Sometimes discouragement settles on my head. Sometimes the enemy has me bound in the weaknesses of the flesh, and trials by fire seem seven times hotter than normal. Yet that is not going to stop me from praying and reaching out to the lost!

A few portions from David Brainerd's diary helped me. After noting the date, he often recorded something like,

"Had the help of God today in prayer...prayed for two hours." The next entry also gave the date and remarked, "Heavens seemed as brass...didn't have the help of God."

His experience allowed me to understand my ups and downs in prayer. When I seemed to be pushing a wheelbarrow of concrete uphill and time stood still, I probably lacked the assistance of God. When prayer was a pleasure and an hour or so flashed by, I must have had the help of God.

Now I plead for the help of the Holy Spirit, that I might "pray *in* the Spirit."

> *Likewise the Spirit also helps in our weaknesses. For we do not know what we should pray for as we ought, but the Spirit Himself makes intercession for us with groanings which cannot be uttered.*
>
> (Romans 8:26)

Seeking Souls for God

Seek God for souls as never before; then, with equal zeal, seek souls for God. Lift up your voice as a trumpet; spare not. Cry out with Hosea, *"What will you do in the appointed day?"* (Hosea 9:5). Warn them to flee from the wrath to come.

Use the Law of God like an earthquake to shake their sandy foundations. Strip the sinner of every false hope and every fig leaf of self-righteousness. Let the thunder of Sinai strike terror in his heart. Make the commandments so real that he touches the very mountain on which they were given, then thrust him through with the dart of the Word of God.

Show him that he will not escape if he turns away from Him who speaks from heaven. Let the blackness of death consume him until he calls for light, and like the trembling Philippian jailer cries, "What must I do to be saved?"

In regard to using the Law in evangelism, be as the Bereans, who *"searched the Scriptures daily to find out whether these things were so"* (Acts 17:11). If it isn't, burn this book, and mark me as a heretic. Then do the same with the writings of the apostle Paul, Wesley, Spurgeon, Finney, Moody, and Whitefield. But if God's way is to use the Law as a schoolmaster to bring sinners to Christ, then let this truth burn in your heart. Kindle its holy flame.

If the Law is the "key of knowledge" to effective evangelism, pick it up from the pages of Scripture. Then, as God gives you opportunity, try it in the hearts of men. Twist and turn it. Then listen as a seared and dormant conscience falls in line with its golden dictates. Watch in wonder as the door upon which the Savior has knocked opens to let the light of the glorious Gospel of Christ shine on the sinner's darkened soul.

Once you have seen that the *"law of the LORD is perfect, converting the soul"* (Psalm 19:7), grip it with an iron fist, and run in zeal according to knowledge. Then, by the grace of God, you and I will see revival together.

Appendix
Questions and Answers

1. How do you answer someone who says that you are laying a "guilt trip" on him when you use the Law?

Ask, "Which commandment makes you feel guilty? You shall not kill, you shall not steal, you shall not commit adultery?" Then ask him if he can work out why he feels guilty. The Law (when used lawfully) condemns only law-breakers.

2. Won't using the Law make the sinner angry?

Yes, it may. Imagine taking a small child to the doctor because he gashed himself on a rusty nail. Suppose the doctor makes the following statement: "This child will die if he doesn't have a tetanus shot right away. I must inject it directly into the wound. Obviously this will cause tremendous pain to him, so I think it would be better for us to let the child die."

If that doctor cares for the welfare of the child, he will say, "This injection is going to hurt your child. It will make him scream. He may hate me for doing this, but it will save his life. Now hold him still while I inject the wound."

If you and I really care for the eternal welfare of the sinner, we will pray, "Dear God, please hold him still for me. Give me courage to pierce his flesh with the needle of the Law, so the medicine of the Gospel can save his soul." If we discard the needle for fear of causing him pain, the medicine of the Gospel will run off his flesh—like water off a duck's back—and he will die in his sin.

Faithful are the wounds of a friend. (Proverbs 27:6)

Don't let angry reactions concern you. A dentist knows that he is in the right place when he touches a nerve. Anger in the heart of a sinner means you've exposed his sin and struck a raw nerve. Anger is a thousand times better than apathy. Anger is a sign of conviction.

Read Acts 19 and see how the apostle Paul was a dentist with an eye for decay. He probed raw nerves wherever he went. At one point he had to be carried by soldiers because of the "violence of the people." (See Acts 21:36). Now there's a successful preacher! He didn't seek the praise of men.

John Wesley told his trainee evangelists that when they preached, people should either get angry or they should get converted. No doubt he wasn't speaking about the "love, joy, peace Gospel." Wesley preached sin, Law, righteousness, holiness, judgment, and hell.

3. Should I use all Ten Commandments when witnessing?

If Jesus saw fit to use five commandments in dealing with the rich young ruler, how much more do we need to use all ten! The sinner is far more likely to surrender if he looks down the barrels of ten cannons, rather that just one or two.

4. What if I don't see any obvious results?

Don't worry if you don't see visible results. When the apostle Paul reasoned with Felix, the Bible says that Felix trembled. Paul may not have seen him tremble. Maybe Felix's lip quivered, or maybe his false assurance was inwardly shaken. Paul may have left discouraged. He may have thought, "I didn't do much good, did I?" Felix's lack of response, however, certainly did not keep Paul from preaching the Law of God at his next opportunity.

Like the apostle Paul, I have seen sinners physically tremble and yet turn down the offer of salvation. Don't get discouraged! You can stand on the promise that God's Word will succeed in the matter for which He sent it. (See Isaiah 55:10–11.)

A young man once told me that I spoke to him two years earlier about his salvation. While everyone else was soft with him, I was "heavy" (I had just taken him through the Law). He said, "It's taken two years, but now I am a Christian, praise the Lord!"

5. What part do apologetics play in evangelism?

Apologetical arguments are legitimate bait to use when fishing for men. But if you witness solely in that realm, you may just end up with an intellectual decision, rather than a repentant conversion. The sinner will merely acknowledge that God is real, Jesus is Lord, and the Bible is the Word of God—but even the devil knows that.

Go fishing without the hook of the Law, and you will end up with plenty of nibbles, fat fish, and no catch.

6. Where do signs and wonders fit into the use of the Law of God?

John Wimber, in his book *Power Evangelism,* quotes the following statement made by Peter Wagner:

The main function of [signs and wonders] is to draw attention to the power of God in order to open the unsaved people's hearts to the message of the Gospel.

Signs and wonders may grab a man's attention, but the Law brings the knowledge of sin. Miracles are the bait, but the Law is the hook. If you get a "conversion" on signs and wonders alone, you may end up with a "Simon the magician" convert. He saw signs and wonders and believed to a point of water baptism (see Acts 8:13), but Peter discerned that he was still in the *"gall of bitterness, and in the bond of iniquity"* (Acts 8:23 KJV).

I recently spoke with a pastor who had been actively involved in mass crusades in India. Thousands reportedly came to Christ through these miracle crusades, but my fears were confirmed when he admitted, "Go to India and look for them...they are nowhere to be found." These healing crusades attract multitudes who make a decision because they have seen the power of God manifested in some way, but they are not warned to flee from the wrath to come.

As human beings, we tend to be so impressed with power that we forget the command of Scripture to look for fruit. I have personally known a preacher who manifests incredible gifts of the Spirit in the area of power evangelism. At the same time he was moving in the gifts, however, he was committing adultery.

God's gifts are not conditional; if they were, they wouldn't be "gifts." If a Christian sins, God doesn't take the gift back. The gift is not God's; it belongs to the person to whom He gave it. Because of this, we are told to be wary of false prophets, especially in the last days.

> For there shall arise false Christs, and false proph-
> ets, and shall show great signs and wonders; inso-
> much that, if it were possible, they shall deceive the
> very elect. (Matthew 24:24 KJV)

These warnings should give us a discerning, sober, and soul-searching attitude to miracles, whether they come from our own hands or the hands of a preacher. What's more, these thoughts should cause us to see that signs and wonders are not shortcuts to the sinner's salvation, but the way of entry into his heart to use the Law as a schoolmaster to bring him to Christ.

7. Can I preach repentance without preaching the Law?

Some preach repentance without the Law. (I say "some" because in this day and age, repentance is a refreshing word.) The first words of Jesus' public ministry were to repent and believe in the Gospel. (See Mark 1:15.) John the Baptist also preached repentance. But remember, the ministry of John the Baptist was to Israel, and Jesus was *"not sent but unto the lost sheep of the house of Israel"* (Matthew 15:24 KJV).

Israel already had the Law. The Law prepared the way for John and Jesus to preach repentance. To preach repentance to those who are oblivious to sin is like trying to save a man from drowning, when he doesn't believe he's drowning. The Law reveals the need for repentance.

8. What do you do if a person's motive is wrong?

I normally open with an anecdote or apologetics until I get listeners, then I preach the Law, grace, and repentance. If people respond, I ask potential converts why they want to follow Christ. If a sinner is lonely, wanting peace or love, he has a wrong motive. He should be coming to Christ solely to flee from the wrath to come. His attitude should parallel the repentance that David demonstrated in Psalm 51.

If a sinner lacks conviction, I take advantage of the situation to appeal to his conscience using the Law. Conscience literally means "with knowledge." When he lies, he does it with knowledge that it is wrong. When he steals, he does it with knowledge that it is wrong. He knows in his heart that God should be first in his affections.

9. Is it right for a sinner to come to Christ through fear of the Law?

Yes, because the Law produces *legitimate* fear, showing us that we deserve punishment. A drug dealer in a country that exercises the death penalty will fear when the law knocks on his door—and rightly so! The knowledge of his guilt produces legitimate fear. The Law awakens the sinner to the real danger he is in because of sin.

10. Should pastors preach the Law on Sunday morning?

I am often asked by pastors whether or not they should preach the Law to their congregation. If the people are unconverted, the answer is yes. But if you have a congregation of Christians and you lay the Law on them, you will drive them away. The Law is *"not made for a righteous man, but...for sinners"* (1 Timothy 1:9 KJV).

If you challenge sinners at the end of your sermon, use the Law before grace, and make sure your people know why you do so.

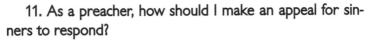

11. As a preacher, how should I make an appeal for sinners to respond?

Make an appeal by using what I call "cold-turkey altar calls." I hold back the musical trimmings and appeal to the will and the conscience rather than the emotions. I think music has legitimate use, but only after the initial appeal has been made.

Ministers experience tremendous peer pressure to get "results" at the altar. Don't let this pressure make you fall back into modern methods. Little or no response at the altar does not necessarily indicate failure.

God is not confined to the front of a church building. If you have preached the truth in love, God will watch over His Word. Let your praise be of God and not of men.

12. How do I deal with backsliders in reference to the Law?

Usually those who have backslidden never slid forward in the first place. Jesus said if we put our hand to the plow and even look back, we aren't fit for the kingdom of God.

Backsliders don't just look back, they *go* back—so something was radically wrong. I gently tell them that they had a false conversion (see Mark 4), then I take advantage of their openness to take them through the Law.

13. How do I witness to intellectuals?

When it comes to intellectuals, don't be fooled into going for the mind; go for the conscience.

I recently heard of a farmer who found fourteen of his cows dead because of "bloat." His cows, which cost him $640 each, ate the wrong feed, became puffed up, and died.

The tragedy was that, had he known better, he could have saved them by piercing the cow between the ribs with a sharp knife. This is a common practice with farmers; the cow immediately comes back to size like a deflated balloon.

Knowledge puffs up the intellectual, but the Christian can pierce his conscience with the sharp instrument of the Law and bring him back to his right place before God.

The same principle applies to most of the "hedges" used by sinners. Answer their questions to the best of your ability, but always bring them back to their responsibility to God on Judgment Day. If you are stumped by a particular question, don't be too proud to admit that you don't know. Be willing to investigate and get back to them.

14. Should I lay the weight of the Law upon someone who has already had a life of tragedy?

Answer me this. Do I fail to warn someone in the plane about the jump because he has a sore foot? No, I just pray that his pain doesn't distract him from the sobering message I have for him.

15. Should I talk about death and dying?

I am a firm believer in appealing to the sinner's will to live. The Scriptures tell us that God has *"put eternity in their hearts"* (Ecclesiastes 3:11). Unfortunately, we don't realize the strength of our will until someone tries to take our life away. For example, people diagnosed with terminal diseases suddenly discover how strong that will is.

Make a legitimate appeal to this ally of the Gospel. I find the most hardened sinner nodding in agreement with me when I speak of the futility of attaining love, laughter, and all the pleasures of life only to have them ripped from your hands by death.

I appeal to his sense of reason, so that he might open his heart just to listen to the claims of the Gospel. That often makes it possible to precede the Gospel with the Law.

About the Author

Ray Comfort has spoken in approximately 700 churches, from almost every denomination. His ministry has been commended by Dr. D. James Kennedy, Bill Gothard, David Wilkerson, and many other Christian leaders. He has written extensively on evangelism, including writing for Billy Graham's *Decision* magazine and Bill Bright's Worldwide Challenge. His literature is used by the Moody Bible Institute, Leighton Ford Ministries, Institute in Basic Life Principles, and the Institute for Scientific & Biblical Research. He has written more than 35 books and is a regular platform speaker at Southern Baptist State Conferences. His videos were seen by more than 30,000 pastors in 1992.

If you would like to receive a free monthly e-mail newsletter from Ray Comfort, send an e-mail with your e-mail address to newsletter@raycomfort.com.

http://www.raycomfort.com

Suggested Reading

Alleine, Joseph. *Alarm to the Unconverted.* Carlisle, PA: Banner of Truth, 1979.

Brainerd, David. *David Brainerd's Personal Testimony.* Grand Rapids, MI: Baker Book House, 1981.

———. *The Life of David Brainerd.* Grand Rapids, MI: Baker Book House, 1979.

Bunyan, John. Grace Abounding to the Chief of Sinners. New Kensington, PA: Whitaker House, 1993.

———. *The Pilgrim's Progress.* New Kensington, PA: Whitaker House, 1973.

Coleman, Robert E. *The Master Plan of Evangelism.* Old Tappan, NJ: Revell, 1979.

Finney, Charles. *Experiencing Revival.* New Kensington, PA: Whitaker House, 2000.

———. *Revival Lectures.* Old Tappan, NJ: Revell, 1979.

Foxe, John. *Foxe's Book of Martyrs.* New Kensington, PA: Whitaker House, 1981.

Johnstone, Patrick. *Operation World.* Waynesboro, GA: STL Books, 1986.

Kennedy, Dr. D. James. *Evangelism Explosion.* Wheaton, IL: Tyndale House, 1970.

Last Days Collection. Lindale, TX: Pretty Good Publishing.

Lawson, James Gilchrist. *Deeper Experiences of Famous Christians.* New Kensington, PA: Whitaker House, 1998.

Lehmann, Danny. *Bringin' 'Em Back Alive.* New Kensington, PA: Whitaker House, 1987.

Little, Paul. *How to Give Away Your Faith.* Downer's Grove, IL: InterVarsity Press, 1979.

Moody, Dwight L. *The Best of Dwight L. Moody.* Grand Rapids, MI: Baker Book House, 1984.

Murray, Andrew. *Raising Your Children for Christ.* New Kensington, PA: Whitaker House, 1984.

Peretti, Frank. *This Present Darkness.* Westchester, IL: Crossway Books, 1986.

Peters, George W. *Saturation Evangelism.* Grand Rapids, MI: Zondervan, 1970.

Petersen, Jim. *Evangelism as a Lifestyle.* Colorado Springs: Navpress, 1981.

Pink, A. W. *Eternal Punishment.* (booklet)

Pippert, Rebecca. *Out of the Salt Shaker and into the World.* Downers Grove, IL: InterVarsity Press, 1979.

Pratney, Winkie. *Revival Principles to Change the World.* New Kensington, PA: Whitaker House, 1983.

Ravenhill, Leonard. *Revival God's Way.* Minneapolis: Bethany House Publishers, 1983.

Ryle, John Charles. *Old Paths.* Greenwood, SC: Attic Press, Inc., 1972.

Smith, Chuck. *What the World Is Coming To.* Costa Mesa, CA: Word for Today.

Spurgeon, Charles H. *The Best of C. H. Spurgeon.* Grand Rapids, MI: Baker Book House, 1986.

Torrey, R. A. *How to Bring Them to Christ.* New Kensington, PA: Whitaker House, 1981.

———. *How to Witness to Anyone.* New Kensington, PA: Whitaker House, 1986.

OTHER POWERFUL Books
from Whitaker House

How to Bring Them to Christ
R. A. Torrey

We often find ourselves overwhelmed with fear, uncertainty, and rejection in our clumsy attempts to witness. R. A. Torrey's personal examples and practical soul-winning principles will give you confidence and enable you to find your true Source for telling others about Christ—our Lord Himself.

ISBN: 0-88368-641-1 • Pocket • 154 pages

Raising Your Children for Christ
Andrew Murray

In this practical guide to parenting, Murray shows the essential qualities of being a parent who loves the Lord. You will find advice and God's promises on how you can shape and mold the lives of your children for eternity.

ISBN: 0-88368-045-9 • Pocket • 312 pages

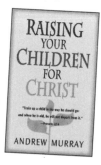

How to Witness to Anyone
R. A. Torrey

Here is a valuable ministry tool that will teach you how to use God's Word to become a successful soulwinner. This easy-to-use handbook quickly points to the Scriptures that answer the questions and settle the doubts of people who have not yet met Christ.

ISBN: 0-88368-170-6 • Pocket • 111 pages